SATANISM AND CULT RELIGIONS

The Studies Of Satanic Strongholds In Relation With Missing People Who Are Used As Ritual Sacrifices

Dipo Toby Alakija

© Copyright 2019 by Dipo Toby Alakija

Printed In The United States

All rights reserved by Calvary Rock Publishing in Nigeria. No part of this book may be reproduced or transmitted in any form or by any means without written permission of the publisher through the address below.

ISBN: 978-978-0650-438

Published In 2019 By
CALVARY ROCK PUBLISHING

19, Ajina Street, Ikenne Remo,
Ogun State, Nigeria.

INTRODUCTION

The International Tribunal into Crimes of Church and State (ITCCS) was founded in May, 2010 at a closed door meetings of survivors of Church and State terror in Dublin, Ireland. The event was initiated by Reverend Kevin Annet, a Nobel Price Nominee and member of Irish survivors' group.

The main purpose of ITCCS is to unite survivors of genocide and child torture across borders and to mount a broad political, spiritual and legal movement to disestablish the Vatican and other Churches and governments responsible for historic and ongoing crimes against children and humanity.

The original ITCCS federation was composed of groups from Ireland, England, the United States, Canada and Italy - Templemore Forgotten Victims (Antrim, Ireland), The Friends and Relatives of the Disappeared (Canada), and the United against Church Terror (USA). By September, 2013, ITCCS had grown so popular that it has spread to twenty-six countries and with over fifty affiliated groups, which include prestigious Cult Ritual And Abuse Survivors' Organization (SMART) of the United States.

One of the most celebrated cases handled by ITCCS implicated Pope Francis. The news on Monday, October 28, 2013 has it this way: The criminal prosecution of yet another Pope came closer to reality this month as Italian Politicians agreed to work with the ITCCS in Common Law Court action against the Papacy for its harbouring of a wanted fugitive from justice: deposed Pope Benedict, Joseph Ratzinger.

The agreement came after a new eyewitness confirmed the involvement of Ratzinger in a ritual child sacrifice in Holland in August of 1987.

"I saw Joseph Ratzinger murder a little girl at French chateau in the fall of 1987," stated the witness, who was a regular participant in cult ritual torture and killing of children. "It was ugly and horrible, and it didn't happen just once. Ratzinger often took part. He and (Dutch Catholic Cardinal) Alfrink and (Bilderberger founder) Prince Bernhard were some of the more prominent men who took part."

This new witness confirmed the account of Toos

Nijenhuis, a Dutch woman who had gone public with eyewitness account of similar crimes, involving Ratzinger, Alfrink and Bernhard.

Soon after his historic resignation from the office of Catholic Pope on February 11, Joseph Ratzinger was convicted of crimes against humanity on February 25, 2013 by Brussels - based on International Common Law Court of Justice, and a global citizen arrest warrant was issued against him. Since then, he has evaded arrest within Vatican City under a decree of the present Pope Francis.

With the above case and so many cases both known and unknown, Satanism and cult religions have become the order of the day. Since most governments all over the world are implicated, it is becoming more and more difficult if not impossible to convict ritual killers like Ratzinger. According to Henry Makow who had made extensive research on Satanic Ritual Abuse (SRA), cults have infiltrated governments, judiciaries, media and academia. This points out reasons for cover ups. So many cases which were strong enough to get the attention of the court had been swept under the carpet but this, of course, does not conceal the truth. The cases are like half buried corpses. A lot of them are not reported by victims of SRA for the fear of not being believed. In 1996, 300,000 Belgians marched to protest against government cover-ups in Dutroux affair, which involved SRA and multiple child murders. In 1999, a brave and committed young woman called Dr. Reina Michelson exposed an untouchable pedophile and satanic network operating in Australia, which involved high government officials, leading politicians, television executives, top TV presenters and police. In 2011, Netherlanders protested against their government's cover-up of senior politicians Joris Demminks' raping, torturing and murdering of boys. In 2012, it was revealed that deceased UK celebrity Jimmy Savile, a close friend of the royal family had abused hundreds of children, practiced necrophilia (sex with dead bodies) and attended satanic rituals.

According to Henry Makow, Satanic crime families are adept at hiding - they have hidden in plain sight for centuries. There controlled mainstream media uses the term "satanic panic" to mock survivors and believers, whom they label paranoid crazies incapable of "critical thinking." Evidence of satanic atrocities is rubbished and stories killed.

Some of the sure sighs of Satanism and cult religions include but not limited to the use of foul languages, hate campaigns, misinformation, deception, lies or propaganda which are all intended to mislead people away from the truth.

The results of the research work into Satanism and cult religions will uncover some cover-ups of worshippers of Satan and cult religion practitioners, some of which appear good or even godly on the outside but the inside are full of crimes against humanity.

CHAPTER ONE

CLASSIFICATION OF DEVILS

Dr Faustus says that if he has as many souls as there be stars, he'd give them all for Mephistopheles!

This is a typical thinking of a Satanist, which invariably drive them into getting people initiated into Satanism. Before considering the general steps which people take before getting involved in Satanism, it is crucial to note both biblical and Satanic classifications of devils and then consider the similarities.

Biblical Classifications Of Devils

The Bible (NKJV) says in Ephesians 6: 12, *"For we do not wrestle against flesh and blood, but against principalities, against powers, against the rulers of darkness of this age, against spiritual hosts of wickedness in the heavenly places."* From this above passage, Satanic organization which are not physical are in the following hierarchy:

<u>Principalities</u>: This can be considered as level one or base level of Satanic kingdom or kingdom of darkness. The spirits operating at this level are usually connected with human bodies, emotions and spirit beings, going by the epistle of Paul, the Apostle to the Galatians, chapter 5 verses 19-21. The passage in the Bible listed works of the flesh which can be linked directly or indirectly to principalities. They are sexual immoralities, uncleanness, lewdness, idolatry, sorcery, hatred, contentions, jealousies, outburst of wrath, selfish ambitions, dissentions, heresies, envy, murders, drunkenness, revelries and like.

<u>Powers:</u> This can be considered as the level two spirits in the kingdom of darkness. Just like the rest of other higher levels, these spirits are indirectly linked to human beings. The spirits give human beings supernatural powers to operate beyond human limitations such as the use of magic or other black powers. Any human who is linked with these spirits can operate like a witch, wizard or magician.

<u>Rulers Of Darkness</u>: Those in this category can be considered as level three spirits in the kingdom of darkness.

4

They actually rule the affairs of man over the world and carries out plans of the spiritual hosts of wickedness. These spirits possess or influence leaders in all walks of life, including politics, economics, religions, education and other positions that can influence or carry out the plans of the spiritual hosts. This is one of the reasons most of the leaders all over the world belong to one secret cult or the other.

<u>Spiritual Hosts (Of Wickedness)</u>: This level can be considered as the highest in all the categories of spirits in the kingdom of darkness although it may be subdivided or categorized into different cabinets. In other to confine analysis within the Biblical explanation of the hierarchy of kingdom of darkness, which is the final authority that establishes Christian perspective, it must be concluded that this is where Satan or Lucifer is categorized.

Explanations Of Satanic Classification Of Spirits

According to Satanheaven, which claims to be an authority in the hierarchy or classification of the devils, the first in the order is Beelzebub, the prince of the seraphim who is next to Lucifer of all the chiefs of the nine choirs of the fallen angels. Of the choir of seraphim that fell at first are Lucifer, Beelzebub and Leviathan, who did all revolt. Michael was the first that fought Lucifer, and the rest of the good angels followed him but he (Michael) is the chief among them. (There is a Biblical basis for this claim in the books of Daniel 10: 13, 21, Jude 9 and Revelation 12: 7-9). Beelzebub is mentioned in Matthew 10: 25, 12:24-27).

The second in hierarchy, according to Satanheaven is Leviathan, the prince of the same order with Beelzebub. He is the ring leader of the heretics, tempting men with sins that are directly repugnant faith. (See Psalm 104: 26. Leviathan might have actually been sent to tempt Job to sin since he mentioned his name in the book of Job 41: 1 after the attack in Job 1: 6-22.)

The third in hierarchy is Asmodeus who burns with desire to tempt men with his swine of luxuriousness. He is the prince of wantons. (The only Biblical basis for this demon if it exists at all, going by this description, is in Ephesians 6: 12 which classifies it under principalities.)

The fourth in hierarchy is Balberith which Satanheaven

considered as prince of the cherubim. He tempts men to commit homicides, to be quarrelsome, contentions and blasphemous. (Again, the descriptions of this spirit place him under Biblical classification of principalities.)

Astaroth is next in hierarchy. According to Satanheavens, he is the prince of the thrones who is always desirous to sit idle and be at ease. He tempts men with idleness and sloth. (The Biblical Astraroth is deity of idolaters which can be found in 1 Samuel 7: 3-4 and 31: 10 but going by the description above, this spirit falls into the category of principalities.)

Verrine is next to Astaroth in hierarchy. He is also of one of the thrones that tempts men with impatience. (Verrine if it exists can also be categorized under principalities.)

Gressil is the third in the order of thrones. He tempts men with impurity and uncleanness. (Definitely, if there is any spirit by that name, it falls under principalities.)

Sonneillon is next in the order of Thrones who tempts men with hatred against their enemies. (This spirit falls under Biblical category of principalities.)

Carreau is said to be prince of powers who tempts men with hardness of heart. (This still appears to be in the Biblical category of powers if this spirit exists since it has power to control the hearts of men.)

Carnivean is also said to be in the prince of powers who tempts men with obscenity and shamelessness. (This spirit also falls under Biblical category of principalities.)

Oeillet is said to be prince of dominions which, according to biblical classification, falls under rulers f darkness. If this spirit exists, according to Satanheavens, it is able to tempt men to break the vow of poverty. It, therefore, has the power to control the economy.

Rosier is second in order of dominions he tempts men to fall in love with his sweet and sugared words. (If this spirit exits, it also falls under Biblical category of powers if it actually has power to hypnotize people through the use of words.)

Verrier is said to be prince of principalities who tempts men against the vow of obedience. (This spirit also falls under Biblical category of principalities, going by Satanheavens' descriptions.)

Belias is said to be the prince of the order of virtues who tempts men with arrogance. (There is no Biblical classification of order of virtues because devils do not have what to be considered virtues. Going by the description of this spirit, it falls under either principalities or powers.)

Olivier is said to be prince of the archangels who tempts men with cruelty and mercilessness toward the poor. (By this characterizations and name, this spirit falls under Biblical classification of hosts of wickedness who work directly with Satan or Lucifer.)

Iuvart is said to be the prince of angels. (This probably falls under hosts of wickedness as well.)

Having juxtaposed the classification by the opposite groups which are Christians and sorcerers, it is save to conclude that there are various types of spirits both known and unknown that possess or depress or oppress mankind. In fact, man has never been on his own. He is either depressed or oppressed or possessed by one spirit or the other. Hence the influence of spirits on mankind can never be over emphasized and their operations are too complex for man to comprehend. Listing the names of demons and their operations alone will take eternity. So there is need to limit the focus of the studies only on Satanism and cult religions. Even then there is no single research works that can cover the vital parts of the studies. Thus, apart from relying on cases that are studied, the results of the research works of other researchers are essentials for studies about Satanism and cult religions.

The first case that gives insight into Satanism which is to be considered is that of a former Satanist that goes by the name Samuel Butler. His article was originally posted on December 15, 2009 at Craig's list Seattle.

Samuel Butler asked this important question in the article: *"How well do you know people?"* He went on to say, *"many people think a Satanist will stick out like a sore thumb. Some do, most do not. Just look at Robert Yates* (serial killer from Spokane, Wa.) *He looked normal as did Bundy. Right? Yates was a Deacon in his Church too, by the way. So how do you become wise, spot these people and not a victim?*

"First, know real Satanist look and dress normal - not like Bikers, or Gothic dress or hippies. The ones that look like

trouble (with tattoos, green hair, body piercing) you do not have to worry about. Unless you are into their drug culture, then watch your back.

"Long time Satanists are serious about hiding who they are. The new ones will brag, and flaunt it like it's cool. The long term ones have skeletons in their closet (as they have done sacrifices already) and are very quiet about it. Generally lower level dabblers are meth, coke dealers. Many drug dealers that are into the occult themselves know people that are (in occult.) And they could set up clients, knowing or unknowing, willing or unwilling. You'd be amazed what a dealer in debt to another will do. Most satanic cults make and sell meth. I'm talking in large qualities and much money is paid to police for protection. Many police are involved in these cults. Usually when you hear of the brutal cop that makes the local news... well guess why.

"Satanic cults are everywhere if you know what to look for. There is one in Roy that is a known compound, guarded by men armed with AR-15 riffles. They use Federal laws on religion and the 2nd amendment on guns to guard their compounds. I know of three just like this in Florida and if you even touch their fence, they'll shoot. No games with these people. These places always have lodging in bunkers underground.

"All satanic cults build large underground bunkers and tunnels. The topside is kept clean, underground is where they keep people and do deeds. No one, even police dare to raid these compounds. Most often these people meet at different locations, depending on the ceremony. Often it may be one head member's home.

"The income of the group determines if they meet in the woods or have a bunkers type compound. Not all live in a compound, of course. Many members are Freemasons and we know how they are about secrets. Many satanic cults support themselves by making things to sell to the public. Things like jewelry, especially crosses that you find in Christians stores. With a nice Christian sounding name, they have front companies. The main reason they do this is deception, as they attach demonic spirits on each piece of jewelry they make during ceremonies. That is why they sell crosses to Christians. I think all of us have seen those *fantasy Dungeons and Dragons castles with orbs, druids and dragons often made of pewter, right? Now you know who makes most of them. Many are sold in places like Disney World, also in stores in the malls that sell weird things and such. So we see they have lots of money.*

"Now the real threat is from clean cut looking Satanists. They have good jobs, careers like lawyers, policemen, clergies, pilots, teachers, day care, neighbours etc. Those are the ones that you watch out for. These people most often find positions and carreers working with children so they can find potentials for ceremonies. And if your child comes up missing, no one would suspect your care worker at say perhaps DSHSL, crisis centre or even child's school teacher. After all they know all about your child and their patterns, even schedule. Instead the police and media will look to put blame on a pedophile on the run, not even suspecting the kidnapped child was a set up by one of these people in charge - members of the same cult.

"Keep in mind 80% of all violent crimes are committed by someone the victims know directly. The odds are all of us know someone or many that are Satanists and we may not even suspect them. (You) shake your head (and say) "no way" just as all friends of serial killers would say when they find out who the person really was. Facts are who really knows anyone that well? Not to be paranoid or scared... just think outside the box here and be safe, not a victim.

"There are an estimated 100,000 or more satanic cults in America. Those numbers sadly are out-dated from 1980s; the numbers are much higher now, of course. But it's not a priority of the F.B.I to track anymore. Police are not allowed to call a ritual murder done to someone as so. There are certain codes for these type of satanic murders. This is a fact, ask any police officer. The F.B.I learned long ago when they mention "satanic cult" in the news people to ape shit over it. So most cases are hidden as just murders by crazy people. But they never mention Satanic cult involved or actual ritual. When kids come up missing, investigate care workers, day-care workers, even teachers all well. Guaranteed someone close to the child knows something.... it's just who exactly. The child was scoped out for ceremonies I bet. I know this is hard, if you lost a child. But the chances are these people had

something to do with arranging it, not some drunken pirate as the media will spin it. Dig into some of these people that work with children, and you may find other cases of missing children they knew. Then figure the odds of it. The reason they do not find most missing people is they don't want to find them and are covering up for these groups. After all satanic cults tell you what they do and what (they) believe in. So why not beat on their doors first when people come up missing prior to the ceremony dates?

"Remember Satanists have rights to practice their religion under federal laws protecting freedom of religion. Most nations now have the same laws put in place since the early 1980s.

"Each satanic cult/ Wicca has 13 people. You do the math... as to how many people they each kill yearly. This is not an option for them, this is their religion, keep this mind. The 100,000 mentioned are just satanic, Nazi death cults, Jewish Ritual Sacrifice (JRS) - Talmudic Jesus only, Mexican Santeria, Voodoo, gang initiations or serial killers.

"Though Satanists dabble with spells and conjure demons during ceremonies, they often can't control demons nor send them back. Remember if they were not getting what they want out of these ceremonies they would quit in time. So this means it is real and they are getting things they desire. Luciferians actually control demons and consider Satanists as very dangerous to them. Luciferians are ancient bloodlines. Satanists are like grunt solders. Either way they all kill people and serve the same master.

"Don't assume the millions missing people every year in American were stupid or easily tricked. But if you keep your guard up with everyone in time, these people will show themselves and trip up.

"Always be careful of new people you meet until you know them well enough. In fact make that very well and always test people to be safe. If not, you or someone you love could become a victim to those Satanists. They almost always choose their victims long before hand. That's a fact. Real Satanists always look normal. They will try to get you to try new things, go to new places all to build trust to get you off guard when the time comes.

"Remember it's the normal looking ones that will harm

you. Keep in mind the real Satanists are pure evil. This is real and understand they will have no pity on killing you or your children. How these cults create monsters in simple, sad and very disturbing. All satanic families are programmed SRA (Satanic Ritual Abuse). This is mind control. Horrible abuse fragments the human mind and causes multiple personalities. Out of shock the human brain creates compartments or places to hide. I am talking about REAL trauma here, not just beatings. The worse things you can think of aren't even bad compared to what their offspring are subjected to. This is needed to fragment their minds early in childhood. Once fragmented, they get into the child's mind by getting them to go into another personality then they abuse that one. In time the child has no safe place to go, even in his/her own mind. This violation of their minds is complicated but once it's done, the children do not even dare think about revolting each personality is found then programmed for different tasks. MPD (Multiple Personality Disorder) do not even know they have other personalities. The level of physical abuse children of satanic cults is sickening not to mention the mental torture needed to create the next generation.

"In these cults, they have breeders and use the babies for rituals. Also all members are one complete family. So all children are violated sexually by most members. Some children (who) do not comply to programming, or refuse to kill animals, are then killed by other toddlers as commanded. By 5, these children have to kill other children then remove their organs. This is when they split personalities in other to deal with the commanded task. By 5-6, they are weeded out. By 10, they are seasoned in killing. In SRA, the only time their children are shown attention and love is on ceremony days. In time these children look forward to ceremonies. This is when they are let out of isolation, get fed well, and shown actual love and affection. Afterward they are isolated again from the world. Again starved, deprived of matter if they ask or cry for it, often for days. This makes them hard and callous in nature. By the time children of Satanists/ Luciferians are 8 or 9, they get used to killing other children usually playmates from school or the neighbourhood. Then they are ready to "recruit" or bring playmates from school to kill. And they will

do this for acceptance and love. This is how they group their children. This is also how these people keep secrets in the family.

"These people are not playing games here and this is very serious stuff. Remember it's not what your religion is, or lack that counts... its theirs that matters as killing you is their religion. Warn others and always keep both guards up always, trust no one new, especially the least likely ones you'd suspect such as clergy, Church members.

"Many Satanists are active Church members. Facts are Freemasons and Satanists donate the most money in most Churches all to gain positions of power and trust. From there they can guide the flock onto the passages they want you to learn and not others..."

CHAPTER TWO

SATANISM AND SATANISTS

With the revelation of Samuel Butler in the previous chapter, there is need to study Satanism and Satanists at a glance for the purpose of general knowledge and understanding of the entire subjects of Satanism and cult religions. First, we have to consider the definition of Satanism.

Satanism, according to Wikipedia, is a broad term referring to a group of Western religions comprising diverse ideological and philosophical beliefs. Their shared features include symbol association with, or admiration for the character of Satan or similar rebellious, promethean and, in their view, liberating figures.

The name of "Satan" which connotes the terms "Satanism", "Satanic" and "Satanist" encompasses wide variety of ideological, philosophical and theological beliefs. Thus satanic groups or cults are quite different from one another although the uses of the same terminologies still apply.

ReligionFacts attempts to classify satanic groups to help people understand what each believes and how each behaves. Not every group performs satanic rituals or participates in satanic worship or reads satanic bible or uses satanic symbols or attends the church of Satan that was established by Anton Szandor LaVey in 1966.

Firstly, not every form of Satanism professes a belief in gods or spirits. While some form of Satanism believe in spiritual entitles, others who maybe atheist or agnostics may have a materialistic world view and in relation of faith and religion.

Satanic spiritualities contend that Satan is god or a chief evil spirit and they pursue interaction with him and other evil spirits. In contrast, these Satanists who are professed atheists and agnostics see Satanism as a philosophical world view and manifesting a particular lifestyle, often characterized by questioning authority. The spiritualists are more likely to perform satanic rituals, while the non-spiritual do not.

Secondly, satanic groups include a wide range of adherents. Some Satanists are teenagers who are dabbling in self-proclaimed diabolical groups and covens. These young people practice Satanism recreationally and their activities often include fantasy role-playing games, heavy metal music with satanic lyrics and use of dugs.

Other Satanists belong to groups whose purpose is less recreational. This type of satanic order is often esoteric and regularly practices occult rituals. It is also populated by adults, not teenagers.

Thirdly, satanic organizations have different purposes. Some are public, while others are private. Public groups are sometimes incorporated as non-profit religious organizations and have tax-exempt status in the United States.

Satanism produces the most literature and is even recognized by the United States military. There are also private groups that largely operate in secret.

Wikipedia to a very large extent buttress the facts in Samuel Butler's revelation but the Christian view of Satanism does not wholly agree with the terms or understanding of Satanism. Hence, there is need to consider the Biblical terms of Satanism as opposed to the idea of Western religions that comprise of diverse ideological and philosophical beliefs.

In Mark 3:22-24, the Bible says, "And the scribes which came down from Jerusalem said, He (Jesus) hath Beelzebub, and by the prince of the devils casts he out devils. And he called them unto him, and said unto them in parables, How can Satan cast out Satan? And if a kingdom be divided against itself, that kingdom cannot stand."

Going by the above passage, Satanism can simply be defined as anything or any act against Jesus Christ. In John 8:44-45, Jesus said to the Pharisees who appeared to represent godliness in those days, "You are of your father the devil, and the lusts of your father you will do. He was a murderer from the beginning, and abode not in the truth, because there is no truth in him. When he speaks a lie, he speaks of his own: for he is a liar, and the father of it. And because I tell you the truth, you believe me not."

With references to these passages, Christian view of

Satanism is everything against Christianity. It is like two opposing kingdoms. While the kingdom of God is light, the kingdom of Satan is darkness. While God is good, devil (Satan) is evil. Christ is the Savour of mankind, Satan is destroyer of mankind. While Jesus Christ gives His followers Holy Spirit, Satan gives his own unholy spirits. While Christ establishes His church, which is the congregation of true Christians, Satan establishes many churches or congregation of Satanists or ungodly people or hypocrites though many with deceptive names. There is Bible for Christians and there are numerous satanic literatures. While heaven is for genuine Christians, hell which is originally created for Satan and other fallen angels is now also for those who follow him, according to Psalm 9:17. Jesus Christ says the truth but Satan speaks lies. The list of words and opposite that depict Christian views of Satanism are endless with hardly anything in common. The only thing that is of intense interest to both Jesus Christ and Satan is mankind.

The story of game of life, which illustrates these intense interests is as follows:

There are two opposing teams who are involved in the game of life in a stadium called The World. The two teams are called The Flesh and The Spirit. This game demands that each team must convert the players in the opposing team to their sides. The Flesh team is made up of professional foul players that are characterized by the spirits of Adultery, Fornication, Uncleanness, Lewdness, idolatry, Sorcery, Hatred, Contentions, Jealousies, Wrath, Selfish-Ambitions, Dissensions, Heresies, Envy, Murders, Drunkenness, Revelries and many others that are opposed to the rules of the game of life called The Bible. (Galatians 5:19-21).

The players in The Spirit team are descent people who play by the rules of the game because they are characterized by fruits of the Holy Spirit called Love, Joy, Peace, Long-suffering, kindness, Goodness, Faithfulness, Gentleness and Self-Control. (Galatians 5:22-23). The result of the game will determine the eternal destinations of all the players, both in The Flesh and The Spirit teams. Whoever plays by the rules of the game will end up getting a mansion in the place of eternal bliss called Heaven but whosoever does not play by the rules will end up in a lake that burns with fire and brimstone called Hell. (Revelation 21:7-8).

In order to ensure that the players in The Spirit team plays by the rules of the game, the Coach called Jesus Christ gives the members a Guardian called Holy spirit who directs them in the way to play. The coach of The Flesh team called Satan or Devil, however, ensures that members of his team do not play by the rules by giving them so many guardians called Unholy Spirits.

Satan not only deceives and manipulates the players in The Flesh team with the use of things they can perceive with their human senses; he also uses them to deceive others in the stadium, teaching them how to violate the rules and how to deceive opponent players. (2 Timothy 3:13).

While players in The Flesh team are constantly seeking to win people in the stadium to their side, strange enough, most of the players in The Spirit team are doing little or nothing about gaining people to their sides. Consequently, the stadium becomes filled with corrupt and foul players.

With the audiences in Heaven and Hell, which are quite invisible to the people at the stadium, there is always joy on the side of The Flesh team whenever a player in The Spirit team falls. Even then also, there is always joy in Heaven if a player in The Flesh team is converted to The Spirit Team, according to what Jesus said in Luke 15:7. He said, *"I say unto you, that likewise joy shall be in heaven over one sinner that repents, more than over ninety and nine just persons, which need no repentance."*

God sent Jesus Christ, His son to give as many as receive Him the power to children of God, according to gospel of John chapter 1 verse 12 while Satan, according to Revelation 12:12, has come down to man with great wrath. Satan does not love any human as many Satanists think but God so love man, according to John 3:16, that He gave his only begotten son (Jesus) so that man may not perish in hell but have everlasting life in heaven. Verse 17 says, *"For God did not send His son into the world to condemn the world, but that the world through him might be saved."*

The world has more problems than any man can imagine but through the study of the Bible, putting their faith in Jesus Christ people can be liberated. There are so many people living or dead whose lives had been transformed through the gospel of Jesus Christ. However, vast majority of people in the world had been enslaved through web of lies that had been created by Satan.

In Matthew 24:24, Jesus said while addressing the disciples, *"for false christs and false prophets will rise and show great signs and wonders to deceive, if possible, even the elect (shall also be decided)."* In other words, according to the prophesy of Jesus Christ, the level of lies and deceptions all over the world will be so much that some Christians shall be deceived.

The web of lies and deceptions have gone to the extent that Satan makes himself appear like Godhead, which was what he tried to do in heaven, according to Isaiah 14:12-14. The plans to send his own christ who will be Anti-Christ is confirmed in 1 John chapter 2 verse 18. The Bible says, *"Little children, it is the last time: and as you have heard that anti-Christ shall come, even now are there many anti-Christs; whereby we know that it is the last time."*

Following the Christian baptism formula in Matthew 28:19 where Jesus told his disciples to make disciplines of all nations and baptize them in the name of the Father and of the Son and of the Holy spirit, Satan makes himself the father, makes anti-Christ the son and evil spirits the unholy spirits.

According to the above passage in John 2:18 and Matthew 24:24, satanic web of lies and deceptions has brought about many cults religions, many of which pose as Christianity. When Jesus said that even the elect shall be deceived, He actually means that there would be some Christians who will turn Satanists either ignorantly or willfully, knowingly or unknowingly and some believing that they are still followers of Jesus Christ whereas they are Satanists. The case of Joseph Ratzinger, Pope Benedict XVI who blended Catholicism with Satanism is a classic example.

Ratzinger was a professor of theology at several German Universities, the last being the University of Regensburg, where he served as Vice President between 1976 and 1977. He was appointed Archbishop of Munich and Freising and cardinal by Pope Paul VI in 1977, which is an unusual promotion for someone with little pastoral experience. From 2002 until his election as Pope, he was also Dean of College of Cardinals. Prior to becoming Pope, he was *"a major figure on the Vatican stage for twenty-five years."* As one of the most respected, influential and controversial member of the College of Cardinals, he had an influence *"second to none when it came to setting Church priorities and directions"* as one of John Paul II's closest confidants.

Going by the claims of Ratzinger's achievements, especially in handling Catholic sex abuse cases, it is easy to believe that he stood firm against Serial Ritual Abuse (SRA). Thus in 2001, he was able to convince John Paul II to put the congregation for Doctrine of Faith in charge of all investigations and policies surrounding sexual abuse in order to combat such abuse more effectively. In his role as head of the CDF, he *"led important changes made in Church law: the inclusion in canon law of internet offences against children, the extension of child abuse offences to include sexual abuse of all under 18, the case by case waving of the stature of limitation and the establishment of a fast-track dismissal from the clerical state for offenders."* The same man who had gone this far to create a reputation for himself as a defender of children was alleged through several eye witnesses that he was involved in ritual torture and killing of children. The Pope was forced to step down, claiming a lack of strength due to his advanced age.

In the history of the Roman Catholic Church, a Pope has never resigned because of infirmity. They are expected to die in the office. On February 1st, 2013, the ITCCS found Retzinger guilty of committing or aiding and abetting crimes against humanity, and of being part of an ongoing criminal conspiracy. On February 4th, 2013, he announced his resignation as Pope. He was alleged to have met with Italian President Giorgio Napolitano on February, reportedly seeking immunity from prosecution. Although both Canadian Government and the Roman Catholic Church have long endeavoured to bury the case, there is a growing body of evidence for a so-called "Canadian holocaust." From 1884 to 1984, at least 150,000 native Canadian children were forcibly removed from their homes and placed in government-funded, Church-administrated residential schools.

After considering series of evidence from various countries, ITCCS concluded that Pope Benedict, (Ratzinger),

Stephen Harper and even Queen of England are complicity in crimes against humanity. The influence of ITCCS, however, is entirely depending upon impetus of the people. The verdict will be ignored by the mainstream media, disavowed by politicians and will not be recognized by police officers.

This appears to confirm Samuel Butter's revelation. With these facts and other finding about Satanism and cult religions, it is instructive to note the followings about Satanists and their religions:

1. Real Satanists dress and look normal. The long-term Satanist, according to Samuel Butler, *"has skeletons in their closets."* The dangerous ones are not the Bikers or Gothic dressed or hippies or the ones with tattoos, green hair or body piercings. The dangerous ones are clean cut looking Satanists, some highly placed with good jobs and careers like lawyers, policemen, clergy, media etc. So it is little wonder that Ratzinger was able to get to the position of Catholic Pope. Going by results of research works, there are countless numbers of Satanic Ritual Abuse (SRA) cases, especially sexual abuse cases among Catholic Priests. This invariably establishes the fact that Catholicism is fast becoming, if at all it has not completely become one of the cult religions in the world.

2. It should also be noted from cases that are studied and Samuel Butler's revelations that the reasons for the missing of millions of people every year around the world can be attributed to satanic activities, using the least suspected places like Church, Temples, underground of private properties as places of sacrifices to Satan.

3. It is also instructive to note that Satanism can be practiced in various ways like religion, profession or career. It can be made public or in secret and spread through medium like media, business, religious and charity organizations. A good example is Lucis Trust, the leading and respectable Britain-based cult that worships Lucifer. Lucis Trust ran a religious chapel at New York United Nations Headquarters called The Temple of Understanding. It was also originally founded as the Lucifer Trust in London in 1923. Lucis Trust associated with UNO is the New York of the British organization. The name was changed from Lucifer Trust to Lucis Trust to make the nature of the organization

less conspicuous. Some of the sponsors of the organization include Supreme Grand Commander of the Supreme Council, 33rd Degree Southern District Scottish Rite Freemasons, The Rockefeller Foundation, The Marshal Field Family, The United Lodge of Theosophists of New York City and a host of others.

4. Satanism is practiced everywhere in the world with no country exempted. Its influence on mankind can never be quantified or overemphasized. The operations of Satanists like Lucis Trust, Freemasons, Illuminati and countless of others have infused all aspects of life from generations to generations. Nearly every culture all over the world has one touch of Satanism or the other. The studies of the operation patterns of the media, politics, economy, social life and entertainments reveal that Satanism and cult religions have infiltrated the society through these means. These invariably condition the minds of the people to accept obscene things as entertainment materials, violence conduct as complementary of peace.

5. The most effect weapons of Satanism are lies and deceptions although in some cases they use threats to get people to comply with their instructions. Typical Satanists will go extra miles to win people's trust. Perhaps this explains reason Lucifer Trust was changed to Lucis Trust. They probably suspect most people would not want to trust Lucifer who has bad reputation as contender with God, going by what the Bible says in Isaiah 14:12-15. It says, *"How art thou fallen from heaven, O Lucifer, son of the morning! how art thou cut down to the ground, which did weaken the nations! For thou hast said in thine heart, I will ascend into heaven, I will exalt my throne above the stars of God: I will sit also upon the mount of the congregation, in the sides of the north: I will ascend above the heights of the clouds; I will be like the most High. Yet thou shalt be brought down to hell, to the sides of the pit."*

6. Satanists always claim to be concerned about humanity. Thus they use many things to entice people. They establish charity organizations, offer benevolent services and create flashy things to cover up their atrocities. They scheme spectacular events to catch attentions, working on the imaginations of mankind through things they can see,

using words like "dream" or "imagine" a world that is free of sufferings, pain or poverty. They create wars and provide means to arrive at peace with the aim of winning people's confidence and trust. When Lucifer Trust was founded with a name like that, Satanists went back to their drawing board and concluded that the name of Lucifer was not appropriate. Many people already identify it as satanic. Hence, it is unlikely to win the trust of many. Samuel Butter said in his revelation, *"many satanic cults support themselves by making things to sell to the public. Things like jewelry, especially crosses that you find in Christian stores. With a nice Christian sounding name (which they know people can trust), they have front companies. The main reason they do this is deception, as they attached demonic spirits on each piece of jewelry they make during ceremonies..."*

6. Every Satanist or those who are inclined into Satanism have been brainwashed, often times possessed with spirits either in the category of principalities or powers or rulers of darkness or spiritual host of wickedness. This explains why some Satanists are more powerful or destructive or dangerous than the others. The other things to note here, based on interviews of the author with former Satanists in Africa are that the more blood sacrifice they are able to make to Satan, the more powerful they become. The more human blood, particularly blood of innocent people like children and their enemies like real Christians they are able to shed, the more they are promoted in satanic ranks. Cases that are studied include the evidence of mass graves of children in Canada, documented by ITCCS, issued to those whose minds are still not clear enough to understand.

In order to understand the various ways Satanists condition the minds of their victims of potential members, there is need to study the gateways to life and soul with the use of the Bible.

CHAPTER THREE

<u>THE FIVE GATEWAYS TO LIFE AND SOUL</u>

The study of the gateways to life and soul is crucial if anyone wants to be on guard against Satanists.

Through this study it would be easy to see how Satan and Satanists use these gateways to gain access to the lives and souls of most people, including Christians. It may be a little surprise to note that these gateways are essentially the human senses of perceptions. More often than not, Satan and Satanists use human senses to influence human ways of thinking and ways of life.

<u>The Ears:</u> Using the ears as channels to human minds, Satan makes use of people that are deceived to organize lectures, music and other things; feeding the human minds with subliminal messages or heresies that lead them right into Satanism. The Bible talks about this deception in 2 Timothy 3:13. It says, *"But evil men and seducers shall wax worse and worse, deceiving, and being deceived."* For this reason, the Bible tells all Christians in 2 Timothy 4:4-5, *"And they shall turn away their ears from the truth, and shall be turned unto fables. But watch thou in all things, endure afflictions, do the work of an evangelist, make full proof of thy ministry."*

A reporter says in The Guardian newspaper in an interview with Jeff Hanneman, a Pop Singer in 2013, *"the best part of the interviewing known Satanists is that you can dispense with pop frivolities - what's your favourite colour? Who do you fancy? Etc and get down to the real issues of modern day existence, like... "Do you really rape virgins and sacrifice goats on alters?*

"Disappointingly, the answer is: of course, we bloody don't..

"Worse still, slayer thrash metal's most musically extreme and professionally offensive exponents are in an almost apologetic mood. Via phone from his LA base, Jeff Hanneman is telling me things like, "Now you see punks and long hairs getting together in harmony which is cool.

"Does he really expect me to believe that he's the guitar - wielding maniac who composed and wrote a current single that goes a little something like this:

"Surgery with no anuesthesia / feel the knife pierce you intensely / inferior, no use to mankind / strapped down screaming out to die?"

In a nutshell, the reporter was able to discover the truth about the source of some song lyrics which influence people to rape virgins, sacrifice goats to the devil and even take their own lives. When people, especially young ones often hear songs like this, they begin to unconsciously serve Satan and then, of course become Satanists at that age. With satanic influence, no one should expect human to act human again. In fact, they become so possessed with demons that they do exactly what they are told to do.

The study of the kind of music people, especially young ones often hear can give us a graphic picture of what is going on in their minds, which invariably explains how and why the crime rate all over the world is so high.

To use the ears as gateway to the souls of men, all Satan needs are messengers or Satanists like Jeff, The Beatles, Rihanna, Buoyancy, Lady Gaga and a host of others who have sold their souls to Satan. Satan also has song writers who serve as medium to receive subliminally destructive messages for their fans. With all these in place, songs that make evil look attractive and glamourous are produced. When people begin to listen to these types of songs either through CD player or MP3 or mobile phones or even lap tops, the stage is set for unholy items like evil thoughts and even demons to gain access into their minds, which would ultimately destroy their lives.

Through what people hear on the radio, TV and other places, Satanism is spread everywhere in the world.

Satanic webs of lies are so well built over the years that it makes presentations and acceptances of truths into the brains very difficult if not impossible tasks.

To further explain how human lives, souls, emotions and actions can be influenced by what they hear, the real life experience of a deaf couple need to be considered, which goes thus:

A gang of armed robbers burst into the compound of a set

of flats in Nigeria in the middle of the night some years ago. The couple lived in one of the flats on the ground floor of the building. While every other person living in all the flats was wide awake with panic after several gunshots, the couple was sound asleep, oblivious of the armed robbery. The robbers gained access into all the flats except the couple's and robbed the people of their possessions. They demanded from the people if there was anyone living in the flat on the ground floor. They were told the occupants were stone deaf. The robbers further required how visitors normally got their attention. Again, they were told it was by pressing a bottom by their door. The button was connected to a light that was in their sitting room. Since the couple was asleep, there was no way they could see if the light was on or not. The armed robbers left them alone.

More often than not, what people hear influences their thoughts and actions. Satanists understand this very well. They, therefore, design best way to inflict people with fear through what they hear. Some news reports are actually meant to frighten people and make them submit the control of their lives to Satanists.

The Eyes: This is the most crucial gateway to life and soul of a person. Because the entire body of a person relies heavily on the eyes, it is shortest route and the easiest way gain access to the mind. Science proves that the brain retains much more information that is received through the eyes than other human senses.

Information can readily be recalled from the memory years later as long as it was obtained through the eyes. Although the eyes work with the ears more often than not yet the brain relies more on the eyes. This explains the rationale behind the adage that says, "seeing is believing". So if anyone hears the sound of anything, he or she would like to see who or what makes the sound before the brain can get full information or sense any danger.

Things that address the eyes like symbols, still or motion pictures and some scenarios are always registered in the brain quickly, retaining them in the memory for a very long time. They also have tremendous effects in the way we think or react or live our lives. For instance, there are chances for a man to be more quickly attracted to a beautiful woman than to an ugly one and vice versa.

While teaching about the need to be careful in the use of our eyes, Jesus said in Matthew 5:27-29, *"You have heard that it was said by them of old time, you shall not commit adultery: But I say unto you, That whosoever looks on a woman to lust after her has committed adultery with her already in his heart. And if your right eye offends you, pluck it out, and cast it from you: for it is profitable for you that one of your members should perish, and not that your whole body should be cast into hell."*

Many may assume that the above passage is bit extreme but it is not. In fact, it is a stern warning that the eyes are gateway to your heart, which is your life. Jesus is saying here that if the use of the eyes is the thing that will make his followers to sin against God, it is better to do away with them, even if it means plucking them out of their sockets than to let them take them to hell.

Satan knows how to use the eyes against humanity. So he recruit good looking and young people to spread satanic spirits through sex, seductive dress, still and motion pictures.

A woman traveling in a bus with other passengers was hard pressed as they journeyed on the highway in Nigeria. She requested the driver to park beside the road so that she could go into nearby bush and ease herself. As soon as she got down from the bus, she hurried into the bush and found a place to ease herself. Not far from where she stooped to pee, she saw a very big snake like a python. She was horrified but knew she has to flee from the place. As she hurried to get up and run for her life, the snake turned into a very beautiful lady; gorgeously dressed. She could not believe her eyes as the lady left the place. When she recovered her senses, she ran back to the bus. She asked the rest of the passengers if they observed a beautiful lady coming out of the bush. One of them replied, saying, "we saw her. She waited by the road side over there. A man ridding a jeep picked her up."

The woman screamed and told them what she saw, *"that lady is not human being! She is a snake demon!"*

From the above case which is similar to many other cases that are studied, it is obvious that Satan and Satanists know how to package deaths with beautiful wrappers for all to see and present them to the world. If it was the man that saw the snake turning into a beautiful lady, of course, he would run for his dear life just as the woman attempted to run but because it was a beautiful lady, he picked her up in his car.

Deaths are usually packaged with different glamorous wrappers and dished out to humanity to see either in movies, media and musicals. Hundreds of millions of people, including children and youths had been destroyed spiritually and emotionally through what they see. Most of them who are influenced by satanic items or means of entertainments or education are prepared to become Satanists without knowing it or its consequences.

The initiations into Satanism are always in stages. Satanism is always introduced to young minds through subliminal messages in cartoons, computer games and satanic symbols in movies and musicals designed for youths.

The case to be studied in this regard is that of Rihanna's 2007 music album with the title: "Good girl Gone Bad". There is a track, "Under My Umbrella", which made the album a hit song. A lot of Rihanna's songs have posed so much threats to moral values that some were banned from daytime television in the US then, making many parents very concerned about what their children watch and hear.

Rihanna's songs are so disturbing and so filled with subliminal messages that anyone who understands the havoc they are capable of wrecking on human minds, especially impressionable children and youths, would be troubled. Using umbrella as a cover-up in the video of the track: "Under My Umbrella," the song is actually filled the teachings of Satan and Satanism.

The part of the chorus of the song goes like this: "you can stand under my umbrel - la, ella, ella, eh, eh, eh..." It was repeated several times.

The Arabic and Hebrew meaning of "la" is "No" and the Hebrew meaning of God is "Ella". The critiques make us to understand that they chose their words precisely and now make millions of people all over the world to sing: "No God, No God."

If you look at the video, the song makes lots of references to occult symbols like the pyramid, the so-called all-seeing

Eye and a demon called Baphomet. Other songs by Rihanna like "we found love" and "S&M" were banned from daytime television because they are full of violence, sexuality, nudity and hard drug related scenes that will naturally influence the youths of today.

A lot of people, especially youths do not become violent or addicted to drugs nor become sexually promiscuous without influence. They are actually influenced by musicals, movies and other things they see with their eyes either on TV or social media or things around them. In other words, Satanism filters into lives through what people see at tender age. When young minds get used to this type of satanic items that entertain them, it is difficult if not impossible to change this wrong set of values and perspectives or satanic ways of life as they grow up. In fact, with the spread of Satanism through what people can see, it will take major miracle in the history of mankind before most of them; especially youths can be transformed.

<u>The Mouth:</u> The mouth can be another gateway to soul and at the same time a weapon to construct or destroy. The Bible says in James 3:6, *"And the tongue (the entire mouth) is so set among our members (of the body) that it defiles the whole body, and sets on fire the course of nature; and it is set on fire by hell."*

An African proverb says, *"the way to a man's heart is the mouth."* This implies that if a woman wishes to really win the heart of her man, she must prepare him good food. In other words, the use of the mouth can be a passage of someone's life and soul through what goes inside. If the food is poisoned, of course, it simply terminates that life.

A case study for this is found in one of the author's novels titled: "The vessel of Destruction" which is the result of his research works on witchcraft in Africa.

There is a woman called Diana in the novel though that is not the real name of the person that went through the experience. Her husband's aunty who was an elderly woman was called Oyinda (in the novel). Oyinda who was a top witch and the princess of doom foresaw her death. She sought for ways to relinquish her position in the kingdom of darkness to Diana who was a very responsible and loving wife and mother of two children. Oyinda pretended to be sick and requested Diana who lived with her family in another city to come and visit her. She vowed that she would not eat unless Diana came to see her. Against her husband's desire, Diana went to Oyinda whose messenger had prepared a delicious meal with the aroma that whet Diana's appetite. Oyinda took part of the meal and told Diana to join her. At first she refused, saying the food was not meant for her. When the old woman insisted, coupled with the appetizing aroma, Diana took out of the meal. Through that, witchcraft demons possessed Diana and she began the process of becoming the vessel that would destroy her own family.

This may come as a little surprise but it is instructive to note that through what people eat, some demons have possessed them. Jesus, however, assured those who believe in Him, saying in Mark 16:17-18, *"And these signs will follow those who believes (in Jesus Christ): in My name they will cast out demons, they will speak with new tongues (heavenly or different language); they will take up serpents (such as the ones that attack in the dream or spiritual realm); and if they drink (or eat) anything deadly (spiritually or physically), it will by no means hurt them; they will lay hands on the sick and they will recover."*

There is need to note in the above passage that Jesus implies something more spiritual than physical. He uses a lot of metaphors in His teachings and parables. When He says drink anything deadly, He does not mean that Christians should start eating deadly things. What He means is that if the devils either through the use of their servants or through dreams or spiritual means gives Christians food or drink that is meant to kill or hurt them physically or spiritually, the deadly thing will not have effect on them.

<u>The Nose:</u> Again, this may come as a little surprise that Satanism can be spread through the nose. More often than not, the use of the nose goes first before a person is enticed to take demonic food like in the case of Diana. The nose is also used directly to entice a person to demonic items or to be possessed through pleasant perfume or fragrance.

Jonathan Benson while reporting for Natural News in June 27, 2012 on Lady Gaga's new perfume which was created with the use of blend of human blood, semen, and poisonous extract said, *"if you have ever doubted the truly satanic essence of the infamous Lady Gaga, then you need look no further than her new perfume, which is expected to debut this fall."* According to the Boston Globe and various other sources, the New Gaga's own blood, as well as semen from another unknown donor form part of the contents of the perfume. The blend apparently also contains a highly toxic plant extract that is known to kill humans.

"It could all just be one big demonic publicity stunt to market the ugly black liquid package in an alien-like, egg-shaped bottle held by what appear to be slender claws. But several sources confirm that Gaga literally used her own DNA to create the scent, which included offering up a blood sample that was actually added to the fragrance batch. Where the alleged semen came from, though, is still unknown.

" 'It was taken out of my own blood sample, so it's a sense of having me on your skin,' said Gaga in early 2011 about the perfume. 'I wanted to extract sort of the feeling and sense of blood and semen from molecular structure that is in the perfume, but it doesn't smell like that.

" 'Actually, the perfume smells like expensive hooker.' "

From this report it is apparent that the nose can be used as a gateway to life and soul. There are many cases of people who were lured into Satanism and witchcraft through perfume or fragrance in some demonic items, going by testimonies of those who were once involved.

Based on other results of research works, it is common practice to dedicate items that are used to spread Satanism to Satan before they are sold out to unsuspecting public. Such items include perfumes, cosmetics, clothing and even food.

<u>Sense Of Feelings And Perceptions</u>: This can be explained as a way of feeling or touching something tangible or intangible such as air and water through the body. The case of Lady Gaga in the report about her satanic perfume can be used to illustrate this gateway. In the news, Lady Gaga said, *"it (part of the content of the perfume) was taken out of my own blood sample, so it is a sense (covenant with Satan since she is a Satanist) of having me (not really her but the demon in her) on your skin (inside you if the perfume touches your skin)."* This is a typical modern way of entering into

covenants with Satan as distinguished from the ancient days.

The study of both old and new testaments of the Bible, which literarily means Old and New Covenants will indicate the importance of blood in the making of covenants. Through Moses, God made blood covenant with the people of Israel in Exodus 24:8. The Bible says in the passage, *"And Moses took the blood (of animal after reading the Book of the covenant to them in verse 7), sprinkled it on the people, and said, 'This is the blood of the covenant which the Lord has made with you according to all these words' (that are in the Book of Covenant.)"*

After the crucifixion of Jesus Christ, which indicates that the shedding of the blood of the Lamb of God that takes away the sins of the world, according to declaration of John the Baptist in John 1:29, the New Covenant (New Testament) was established. This naturally abolished the Old Testament form of worship and sacrifice to God. Immediately after the move of God from old to New Testament, Satan fully establishes himself on the Old Testament form, using God's old method of demanding for sacrifices for himself; thereby posing as god. Thus the Old Testament form of worship and sacrifice was made satanic by Satan himself. Many people, including some Christians who dwell on the Old Testament form of worship are actually paying homage to or worshipping Satan, thinking they are serving God.

Lady Gaga's use of her blood sample in her demonic perfume is a way of making people who listen to her songs to enter into real covenants with Satan when it touches their skins. This typically depicts God's method in Exodus 24:7-8. The Bible says, *"And he (Moses) took the book of the covenant, and read in the audience of the people: and they said, All that the LORD has said will we do, and be obedient. And Moses took the blood, and sprinkled it on the people, and said, Behold the blood of the covenant, which the LORD has made with you concerning all these words."*

The sense of feelings and perceptions can be a gateway to life and soul, which most people are not aware of. Hence items like perfume, artificial hair or attachment, jewelry, cosmetics, some clothing and a host of others can be used as a way of making people go into Satanism.

A Satanist who became a Christian revealed that she was once in charge of using human blood as part of the items that are used to make some cosmetics like lip sticks. The case of Lady Gaga substantiates the possibility. Therefore anyone who feels he or she cannot do without using items like that might have allowed Satanism to creep into his or her life. Only with the power of Jesus Christ can anyone be liberated from the influence of Satanism. It is quite unfortunate that ignorance of this spiritual darkness or the way out of it has made so many to adjust to the dark ways of life.

One horrifying fact about Satanism is that once it finds its way into a life or soul through any of the above gateways, it will establish a stronghold in the life of a person. While adjusting to darkness, people go deeper into Satanism until they are completely blind to the point of not seeing or believing the truth in John 1:4-5, which says, *"In Him (Jesus) was life, the life was the light of men. And the light shines in darkness, and the darkness did not comprehend it."*

Ignorance of Satanists who are conscious or unconscious of their involvements in Satanism is what brings about confusion before eventual destructions of their lives. Ignorance of the word of God and the rejection of Jesus Christ in their lives, going by the passage in Hosea 4:6-7 is what takes them deeper into Satanism, which eventually causes their eternal deaths in the lake of fire and brimstone. (Revelation 21:8).

Anyone who wishes to be free from Satanism would need to go on his or her kneels and call on Jesus, who says to everyone, Matthew 11:28, *"Come unto me, all you that labour and are heavy laden, and I will give you rest."* The Bible also says in Romans 10:9-10, *"That if you shall confess with your mouth the Lord Jesus, and shall believe in your heart that God has raised him from the dead, you shall be saved. For with the heart man believes unto righteousness; and with the mouth confession is made unto salvation."*

CHAPTER FOUR

<u>SATANIC STRONGHOLD</u>

As indicated in author's book titled, The Insanity Of Humanity, *"man is not really in charge of government."* No one is in control of his or her life and the world around him or her. The evidences of satanic strongholds uncovered so far implicate most, if not all world leaders. This proves the fact that the rulers of darkness are ruling through most political, religious and other leaders all over the world.

The deep involvements of some world leaders in Satanism and cult religions are established in the studies of the cases of mass graves of children in Canada and other places. As high as the number of these reported cases, they still prove to be the tip of the iceberg.

The background story of the case of Canada as indicated in investigative reports goes as follows:

In late 2011 in Brantford, Ontario, history was made with the uncovering of forensic evidence of the burial of children at the oldest Indian residential school in Canada. Despite subsequent attempts by the Church and Crown of England and their aboriginal agents to discredit and conceal this evidence of their crimes, this first unveiling of mass graves has prompted new disclosures of genocide across Canada. After the first evidence of mass grave near the Anglican-run Mohawk Institute in Brantford was unearthed between September and November, 2011, these agencies that are responsible for the deaths of children mounted an enormous sabotage campaign to stop the big and fog the evidence. This cover-up eventually involved the Archbishop of Canterbury in London, Rowan Williams, the Anglican Primate in Canada, Fred Hiltz and Buckingham palace. The sabotage temporarily halted the excavation of the Mohawk Institute graves but the evidence uncovered so far confirmed that children are indeed buried there.

This evidence reminds the world and substantiated that the Crown of England, the Vatican and the Canadian government are responsible for the deaths of more than 50,000 children across Canada. The evidence includes recording of the digging at Mohawk Institute, the bones and bits of school uniforms that were uncovered along with other corroborating materials.

Earlier on in April, 2011, ten traditional elders of the Grand River Mohawk Nation issued a written invitation to Kevin Annett and the ITTCS to conduct an inquiry on their land into children who went missing at the nearby "Mush Hole": their name for the Mohawk Institute, founded in 1832 by the Crown and Church of England, where records indicate that on average 40% of the children died until it was closed in 1970.

This case and several others serve as proofs that governments all over the world are involved in Satanism. Hence, it is safe to conclude that Satanists hold political, religious, economic and other positions of power, influence and authority all over the world. They use these positions and powers against humanity. How they are able to hold the world captive is a very complex subject of discussion but efforts would be made to present evidence of how they are able to build satanic stronghold in this chapter.

Firstly, it is instructive to note that some people are born into Satanism while some are initiated. Thus there are only two broad way of getting involve in Satanism and cult religions or to become Satanists, which are by (i) initiation and (ii) birth.

<u>INITIATION</u>: To explain this, let us consider how some people dedicated themselves to Satan as explained by a satanic site in their "Frequently Asked Question".

Question: What happens if you make a formal commitment to Satan?

Answer: Satan looks out for his own. Satan gives you an inner strength and you become very strong spirit. (Note: Giving a person strong spirit is an indication that the person is possessed with at least a demon.) Unlike right hand path religions, where adherents are forever praying and searching for their God, Satan comes for you on his own. Many times you feel him. He comes to guide you when you get down, worried, or are experiencing problems. He snaps you into line and directs you as to what you need to do to be focused and happy. (Note: Most Satanists do not really know Satan. Hence they feel he could make them happy. Research indicates that Satanists are the most depressed set of people in the world. Once they are caught up in satanic web, getting out it is very difficult, though not impossible. A case study of this aspect is that of Michael Jackson who tried to warn people of this satanic web in his music titled: "Invisible" before he was eventually sacrificed to Satan.)

The foundation of spiritual Satanism is in your finishing Satan's work upon humanity. This is the goal of the godhead, (as pointed earlier, Satan is regarded by Satanists as godhead) and is accomplished through power meditations. (Note: This is how the initiation begins. A person who is in the process of initiation is first deceived and brainwashed with lies through the gateways to life and souls and then lured into ignorantly requesting demons to possess him or her in the process of meditation.)

Humanity is currently at a very low level spiritually. When you begin to meditate, you experience profound positive changes within lives. Satan and his demons protect you and look out for you as you transform and achieve personal power. (Note: Satan and his demons are made to appear as if they bring positive changes. The results of this research works through interviews prove these claims to be outright lies. In fact, Satan and demons who constantly crave for human blood and ritual sacrifices bring about horrifying experiences. Victims who were almost destroyed and survivors, including children of Satanists provide more than enough evidence against the claim of positive changes in the lives of Satanists.)

With Satan, you have protection that outsiders do not have. (Note: Satanists make Satan appears like a protector against God and against innocent people. To get that kind of protection, they often times have to sacrifice the lives of innocent people, including children. The question now is: who is the enemy here?)

You can advance in powers of the mind and soul as you wish. For outsiders, this can be dangerous. (Note: To advance in satanic powers, according to the testimonies of former Satanists, blood is required. It often starts with the use of blood of animals as sacrifice. After advancing to certain level in Satanism or cult religions, blood sacrifices of innocent people who are often regarded as outsiders are required.)

Satan also gives you knowledge and lead to the straight part without a book." (Note: Satanists do things by the leading of demons that possess them.)

Through Satan you learn to take control of your own lives and destiny instead of being at the Marcy of fate. You learn to heal yourselves, and to fulfill your own desires, using the power of your mind and soul. (Note: many Satanists do not believe demons control them. Some of them do not know they perform magic of healing with powers of demons. They also do not believe that demons control their lives and destinies. That is the reason Satanists can perform magic and do things that are opposed to human natural feelings like a mother killing her own child for ritual without feeling any qualm about it.)

In making a commitment (to Satan), you engage a formal ritual. This done out of freewill. (Note: Top Satanists know that there is nothing like freewill in Satanism. In fact the freewill is taken over by the wills of demons who direct them as they like.)

You are making a choice, as opposed to being dragged off to same Christian church, and reciting canned prayers in front of a bunch of idiots. (Note: No real Christian Church will drag anyone to itself for whatever reasons. God and Christians respect the power to choose between Christ and Satan. Also note that typical Satanists are full of dirty jokes and foul languages. They are usually rude and very abusive. They have no respect for the power of choice that was given to a man by God so as to exercise his freewill.)

The initiation ritual is very personal, unless you decide to have friends participate, or are doing it as part of a group. (Note: There is contradiction in the area of initiation as the Satanists claim. If it is very personal, how come the participation of friends or a group? Actually, there is nothing personal in initiation, especially if the potential Satanist wants to advance in Satanism. Satanism uses one stronghold to grab another one as we are going to see it in some cases that are studied.)

(If you want to be initiated into Satanism), you will need one black, blue or red candles, a sterilized needle or razor, a piece of clean paper, large enough to write prayers. (Note: Actually you are not about to write any prayer request, going by the wordings you are expected to write. It is statements of covenant with Satan. The potential Satanist will put his or her name under the statements. Using the needle or razor to pierce his or her skin so as to get his blood, he or she will use a dry pen, dip into the blood and use it to sign on the paper.)

It is important to bathe before you perform (the ritual). This is done out of respect (homage to Satan). When you are ready, you can light the candle. Take the needle, prick the index finger of your left hand, squeeze some blood out. Sign your name in blood. After reciting the prayers (the covenant statement) either aloud or in your head, fold the paper and let it burn in the fire of the candle. At the end of the ritual, close with the words: "So mote it be" and a big "hail Satan!" (Note: Anyone who follows this satanic instructions invites demons that may at first request for the blood of animals. They will later constantly request for human sacrifices, including the children of Satanists. A case study of a former witch, whom the author came across while writing the non-fiction novel titled: The vessel of destruction" is a classic example.

The story goes thus: A woman joined a group of white witches, expecting it to protect her children against other Satanists or cultists. Instead of that, she was told to sacrifice two or three of the children she was trying to protect. This would prove that she was loyal to Satan. This woman went to a Pentecostal Church where she and her children were delivered from the witches.

A potential Satanist, according to these findings only needs to perform satanic ritual only once before he or she begins to advance. Satanists claim that the ritual cannot be reversed but former Satanists who are now born-again Christians prove them wrong. In fact they are the ones that give most researchers insight into what Satanism and cult religions are all about by exposing it to the public.

SATANISM THROUGH BIRTH AND CHILDHOOD: Unlike the dabblers who are lured into Satanism, if a child is born into a family that practices Satanism, according to the results of research works, it is usually a very traumatic experience for him or her. At early age of four, children of Satanists are tortured, chronically neglected, repeatedly abused and tortured and terrorized.

Some of these tortures which serve as building them into

Satanists include physical torture like being burnt with cigarettes, light candles and hot light bulbs. They are beaten on the soles of the feet tied down, made unconscious by choking, suffocating with a plastic bag, or face submerged underwater, forced to lie naked in the snow or electric shocked.

The sexualized torture includes placing guns in their mouths, sex organ, or anus, making them to hear the chucking sound when the trigger is pulled. There is also family or group rapes with objects or weapons like knife, broom handle, tree branches and kitchen items. They are forced to consume or be smeared with animal or human waste like vaginal fluid, sperm, blood, urine and feces. They are also forced into pornography, bestiality, forced pregnancy and or abortions.

The mind spirit torture includes humiliation, degradation, objectification, treating them like an animal trained to commit suicide. They are programmed to kill themselves if they try to tell anyone. They are drugged and forced to participate in cruelty and killings of pets. They are made to witness the torture of others.

These satanic group or family can be both inter-generational and extra familial.

Child victims are forced into a group bonding process often with the cooperation of their families and forced to take vows and oaths of secrecy. The programming triggers are indoctrinated into survivors when they are children. They are subjected to mind-control programming, using hypnosis, mind-altering drugging and the implantation of trigger messages to prevent them from disclosing their ritual abuse ordeals.

Torture, long-term and repeated pain, deprivation, death threats, harassment and intimidation are used on young victims.

Victims are forced to violate others. There is a case study of a child who was killed by another child because he refused to kill a child victim.

Some of the reasons for these torture is related to mind-control, which according to results of research works is where part of the person's mind had been programmed (trained) to obey another person without question, while other parts of the mind are unaware of this situation.

Programming refers both to the process of teaching part of the mind unquestioned obedience and to the content of what is taught. Thus you can say that a person had been programmed to commit suicide under certain conditions, or you can take a suicide program that is triggered (activated) by certain words or conditions. It is helpful to remember that programming is something that is done to a human being by another human being for a specific reason, using certain time-tested techniques, at a certain time and place.

A person who is programmed, but unaware of this fact can be made to do many dangerous or illegal things. Such persons make perfect spies, for example, because they are unable to reveal their missions if captured. They simply do not know what they did, or what they were supposed to do, and cannot give any information. They would also make good assassins, drug runners, money launderers, sexual slaves for prostitution, pornography, or blackmail or anything that requires secrecy.

The case study that probably buttresses some of these facts are attributed to a Christian woman called Nancy Dun in her testimony titled: "Not What You See." It goes thus:

"On my thirty-third birthday, memories from my childhood opened up like a floodgate. My eight year-old son had just told me that my father had sexually abused him. All at once, long-hidden, painful memories began to unravel in my mind: There I was, lying on a stone alter. Seven men wearing black hooded robes were standing around me, taking turns sexually assaulting and torturing me.

"But how could this be? I had grown up in Central California near the ocean in an average home in an average neighbourhood. My mother worked for a local doctor and my father had a government job with top security clearance. I had a younger brother and a dog named missy. I later became a flight attendant for a major airline.

"My family was living a secret life - my father was a Satan worshiper. As a high priest, he ruled over a large satanic group in California. My father had followed in the footsteps of 25 generations of Satan worshipers in his family... (So) I become a victim of satanic ritual abuse.

"At the age of eight, I had the opportunity to learn about

Jesus and accepted Him as my personal Saviour. A Christian family lived two doors down from our family, and I played in the neighbourhood with their son and daughter. One day, their mom, Pearl Farrington, loaded up with all the kids on the block and took us to her Baptist Church for the "Awana Olympics". It was an exciting day for me because I won a trophy. But for greater than winning a trophy at the event was hearing Mrs Whitestone tell me about Jesus Christ. As she shared that Jesus was God's Son who died for my sins and could give me eternal life, a sense of hope covered me. For the first time in my life I knew there was a way of salvation for me. I know I wouldn't be here today if it were not for Jesus Christ and the obedience of Pearl Farrington and Mrs. Whitestone who made the day possible.

"When the horrible memories from childhood surfaced, a therapist helped me connect with a group of other survivors of satanic ritual abuse. I learned that in order to survive the extreme trauma caused by the abuse, the mind would actually split and compartmentalize the hurtful experiences. When this happens, different personalities hold different memories, and one personality can watch the other from a distance. The resulting condition is called Multiple Personality Disorder (MPD) or Dissociative Identity Disorder (DID). I was able to recognize hundreds of different personalities inside of me. They were all different ages, with different memories, trauma and appearance.

"Often in the darkness of night, my father would take me on the back of his motorcycle on a journey into caves overlooking the ocean where satanic rituals took place. Satanists are an organized group; they even have a satanic calendar, dictating what type of ritual should happen and when. For example, Halloween requires the blood sacrifices of an infant; other dates require the sexual sacrifices of a teenage virgin. They attempt to control and destroy lives through a systematic dehumanization of the soul.

"That first memory of seven hooded men standing round me was my seventh birthday. Because I was born on Easter Sunday, this made me somehow 'special'. They would make of mockery of Christ's resurrection as they abused me on each of my birthdays.

"For many years there had seen a deep grieving in my

soul. I came to identify this grieving as a longing of a mother who was unable to hold her child. I discovered that I was used as a baby breeder. I was impregnated by my father or someone else in the group several times so that I would have a baby that they could use as a human blood sacrifice to Satan.

"The experts say that it takes eight years of therapy for people diagnosed with Multiple Personality Disorder (MPD) or Dissociative Identity Disorder to become integrated. But, within a year and a half after I began therapy, God supernaturally delivered me out of my captivity. One day at Church, as I took communion and observed the elements that symbolize the body of blood of Jesus, the memory of the many times I was forced to drink human blood came rushing back into my mind. In that moment I sensed the Lord's presence strong around me and I heard Him say, 'Trust me, and I will heal you of every foul things that has ever touched your lips.' For about two weeks afterwards, I could see within me hundreds of personalities lined up around a room, coming together and integrating. Then all was quiet within me. My many personalities had become one, and I was whole!"

CHAPTER FIVE

SATANISM IN THE WORLD

According to the results of series of research works that are carried out in different countries, all governments all over the whole are implicated or involved in Satanism, which necessarily makes them commit crimes against humanity.

According to analyst researchers on the issue of Satanism, Governments' involvements in Nazi Germany, Canada, the United State, United Kingdom, Italy and a host of others had been documented either in these countries of by the International Tribunal Into Crimes Of Church And State. Some documents in the US which were originally classified have been declassified. Some papers were published in academic journals and some correspondence has become public. Of course, there are also the testimonies of survivors who have become conscious of what was done to them. Due to the absence of access to mainstream publishing companies, self-published books are a valuable source of information. For instance, some members of the US military who were subjected to mind control experimentation and procedures are legally bound to secrecy.

There is no parallel documentation for the use of mind control in cults, since cults do not keep records the way governments do. If there is a cult paper trail, it has not yet come to light. But we can assume from the testimonies of ritual abuse survivors and behaviours that mind control is widely used in abusive cults and that cults and government network to perfect techniques.

There is a great deal of evidence supporting the existence of Satanism and ritual abuse crimes as a worldwide phenomenon. Bottoms, Shaver and Goodman found in their 1993 study evaluating virtual abuse claims that in 2,292 alleged ritual abuse cases, 15% of perpetrators in adult cases and 30% of the perpetrators in child cases confessed to the abuse.

"In a survey of 2,709 members of the Americans Psychological Association, it was found that 30 percent of these professionals had seen cases of ritual or religion-

related abuse." (Bottoms, Shaver and Goodman, 1991). Of those psychologists who have seen cases of ritual abuse, 93 percent believed that the alleged ritualism occurred.

The similar research of Nancy Perry (1992) further supports (the previous findings). Perry also conducted a national surgery of therapists who work with clients with dissociative disorders. She found that 88 percent of 1,185 respondents indicated *"belief in ritual abuse, involving mind control and programming."*

An online survey of over one thousand people answered questions about ritual abuse and extreme abuse crimes. In a summary of the survey, it was found that ritual abuse/mind control is a global phenomenon. Fifty-five percent of the adult survivors that responded stated they ere abused in satanic cult. Seventy-seven percent of adult survivors that responded *"had been threatened with death if they ever talked about the abuse."* Also, 257 respondents reported that secret mind control experiments were used on them as children. Eight-two percent reported being sexually abused by multiple perpetrators.

Anne Johnson Davis in her book "Hell Minus One" reported that her parents confessed to her abuse in writing and verbally to clergymen, and to the detectives from the Utah Attorney General's office. Her suppressed memories started when she was in her mid 30s, which were fully substantiated by her mother and stepfather.

Many scientific journals articles have discussed the reality of ritual abuse and its effect on its victims. Some of these articles have discussed the extreme nature of these crimes, proof of the reality of the ritual abuse phenomenon and victims' symptoms, the connection between ritual abuse and its effect on its victims. Some of these articles have discussed the extreme nature of these crimes, proof of the reality of the ritual abuse phenomenon on and the victims' symptoms, the connection between ritual abuse, Multiple Personality Disorder and mind control and connections between ritual abuse reports and the higher levels of symptoms of childhood sexual and physical abuse. Several additional studies and organizations have compiled research on the reality of ritual abuse crimes.

A study which identify 270 cases of sexual abuse in day

care settings found that allegations of ritual abuse occurred in thirteen percent of the cases. Additional evidence of ritual abuse in day care and child abuse cases has been found in news reports, journal articles and legal transcripts.

Ritual abuse occurrences have also been found in the Netherland and England.

With so much proofs presented by analysts, journalists, researchers, scientific journals and a host of others; Governments nearly all over the world still find it impossible to tackle this crimes (of Satanism) against humanity. With available evidences, including various documents provided by the International Tribunal into Crimes Of Church and State, there are proofs that there is hardly any Government all over the world that is not involved in Satanism and cult religion.

In their article titled: "The Hard Facts About Satanic Ritual Abuse", Bob and Gretchen Passantino who are Christian researchers into SRA have the followings as their findings:

"A teenage girl who was impregnated during a satanic ritual is forcibly delivered of her nearly term baby and then made to kill the child and eat its heart as cult members watch. Another girl, a small child is sewn inside the cavity of a disemboweled animal and re-birthed by her cultic captors in a grotesque ceremony. A preschool class is systematically abuses sexually, emotionally, and physically - by members of a nationwide, nearly invisible network of Satanic Pedophiles and pornographers. A girl is thrown into an electrified cage with wolves and ritually tortured to deliberately produce a "wolf personality" (as) part of her Multiple Personality Disorder. These are but a few of the thousands of horrifying stories circulating through out the United States and abroad."

Some true believers in Satanic Ritual Abuse (SRA) say that more than 100,000 "adult survivors" have undergone therapy and "remember" these horrible abuses. Others are more than double this number.

These terrifying accounts are linked to the current concern about child abductions by strangers, which claimed to be in thousands annually.

There are allegations of invisible conspiracy which covers nations (if not the entire world). This involves key power players in the courts, education, politics, religion and society in general.

With evidence and unconditional support to alleged adult survivors whose therapeutically recovered "memories" typically implicate their elderly parents in heinous crimes, including murder, cannibalism, sexual torture, incest and bestiality.

Some alleged victims bring their cases to law enforcement officials, hoping for criminal prosecution. Some obtain restraining orders, barring their parents from seeing them or their grandchildren. Some cut all ties with family and simply disappear.

The above findings only substantiate the facts that Satanism and cult religion are in governments, finding its way into politics, education, court of law, economic and social welfare of the people all over the world. With Satanists in governments, it is easy for them to commit all sorts of crimes against humanity and go away with it, making it difficult if not entirely impossible to bring them to justice just like the case of Joseph Ratzinger.

More often than not, Satanists see themselves above the law, if not as gods in the flesh. Hence the long-time Priest in the Church of Satan and media representative in the person of Magus Peter H. Gilmore has the arrogant audacity to say Satanism is a "feared religion". In his article, he says:

"When Anton Szandor LaVey shaved his head and created the Church of Satan on April 30, 1966, he knew that soon he would be the focal point of attention for people throughout the globe. Now that the thirtieth anniversary of the fateful night has passed, has the world begun to understand the real meaning behind the only organized religion in history to take as its symbol the ultimate figure of pride and rebellion, and to many, of Evil?

"And are there truly some grounds for people to feel fear at the ever growing phenomenon of contemporary Satanism? As a long-time priest in the Church of Satan and media representative, I can candidly say, 'yes!' However, what the general populace has decided to fear is a hideous portrait that has been painted in lurid technicolour by media hypesters intent on titillation, evangelists struggling to fill their coffers and keep their mistresses in jewelry, and most distressing, by a segment of the therapeutic community who

have found a gold-mine in the treatment of so-called ritual abuse survivors who provide no evidence of their tales of terror (remarkably similar to stories told by women labelled by Freud as hysterics), save for their fervent belief that they were victimized. I shall not waste time in refitting the absurd claim that there is an international conspiracy of generation Satanists bent on enslaving the world through drug use and sacrifice of babies bred for that purpose by emotionally unstable women. That mythology has been thoroughly explored by other sources (The FBI's national center for the Analysis of Violent Crime: Investigator's Guide to Allegations of Ritual Child Abuse, January 1992; the committee for Scientific Examination of Religion's report Satanism in America, October 1989; the British Government's Department of Health report: The Extent and Nature of Organized and Ritual Abuse, HMSO, 1994)

"Let us instead look at contemporary Satanism for what it really is: a brutal religion of elitism and social Darwinism that seeks to re-establish the reign of the able over the idiotic, of script justice over injustice, and for a wholesale rejection of egalitarianism as a myth that has crippled the advancement of the human species for the last two thousand years. Is that something to fear? If you're one of the majorities of human mediocrities merely existing as media- besotted drone, you bet it is!"

Probably unknown to this ignorant and arrogant Satanist, there are thousands of researchers who have much more information about Satanism than what he could possibly had. Hence, his method of disinformation only adds more to the proofs of the followings:

1. Satanism is involved in serial ritual abuses, including murders of innocent people and children with survivors revealing their secrets.

2. There is Satanism in governments in most part of the world, according to this Satanist buffer's claim that "mythology has been thoroughly explored by other sources" like FBI. With Government agencies involved in any investigation about Satanism, it would be hard if not impossible for the public to know the truth.

3. Evidences of serial ritual abuses, especially sacrifices of children like the one discovered in Canada by International

Tribunal into Crimes of Church and State are being suppressed by the governments.

4. SRA survivors who testified against Satanists established reasons the religion of Satanism and cult religion are feared. Coincidentally, among these survivors is Jess LaVey, the son of Anton Szandor LaVery who founded the Church of Satan. Although, as expected, critics claim that Jess LaVey is not the son of Anton but there are connection of paternity to the founder of Church of Satan who died at the age of 67. While telling his story in Christian Churches, radio interviewers and postings on the internet, Jess LaVey said that he was born in 1968 but not at Satanists' mother Church in East Berlin. He said his father was "a bizarre, sick man" who had raped him and forced him to attend rituals. Jess began to rebel at the age of 10 and later made contact with a Christian Church where at 14 received deliverance from demons. He later graduated from Bible College and founded Sword of the Spirit Ministries. He speaks about the dangers of the occult.

A Christian analyst in his 2006 article titled: Satanic Cult controls (American) Government says, *"More and more illuminati cult victims seem to be coming out with stories so bizarre that most people would dismiss them as total fiction."*

Cathy O'Brien wrote about these things years ago in the book: "Trance Formation of America". *"If her allegations were false why wasn't she sued? Even if 1/10th of these allegations are true, America is in big trouble. But that's nothing new. Even 'beloved' Ronald Reagan was photographed at Satanic Bohemian Grove resort, and he was also photographed giving the Eld Diable Satanic sign. The Bible says Satan controls the kingdoms of this world. He can't control the kingdoms unless he also controls the 'kings'. George W. Bush gave his allegiance to Lucifer at his Skull and Bones initiation, just as his dad did years before, and his dad before that. The Democratic Party (with references to Clinton and Obama Administrations) is no less corrupted by evil...*

"America is a nation mesmerized by TV and a myriad of entertainment forms. How much of Mauri's allegations are true is unknown to us. Certainly with all evidence of government mind-control programs much of it is likely true.

"Mauri had a tough beginning, as she as related it at Greg Szymank's radio show being sold by her parents to an illuminati cult group as a child sacrifice. At the age of three, offered up in a bathtub drowning, she miraculously survived, coming back from the dead on a slab in a cedar city, Utah, morgue. From that day forward, death might have been a better alternative because her life became a living hell."

Also worthy of attention are the books: "Access Denied For Reasons Of National Security", "Trance Formation of America" by Cathy O'Brien with Mark Phillips.

On August 3rd, 1977, the 95th US congress opened her hearing into the reported abuses concerning the CIA's TOP SECRET mind-control research program code-named MK-Ultra. On February 8th 1988, a top-level MK-Ultra victim, Cathy O'Brien was covertly rescued from her mind control enslavement by intelligence insider, Mark Phillips. Their seven years pursuit of justice was stopped "FOR REASONS OF NATIONAL SECURITY". "TRANCE Formation of America" reveals the truth behind this covert government program and its ultimate goal: Psychological control of a nation. It is the first documented autobiography of a victim of government mind control. Cathy O'Brien is the only vocal and recovered survivor of the Central Intelligence Agency's MK-Ultra project monarch operation. Tracing her path from serving as a top-level intelligence agent and White House sex slave, TRANCE formation of America is a definitive eye-witness account of government corruption that implicates some of the most prominent figures in US politics.

With their lives and liberty on the line, "TRANCE" was hurriedly conceded from courtroom testimony into a book form and privately published by the authors in September 1995. "ACCESS DENIED for reasons of National Security" is the rest of their true life story, which required 16 years for the authors to survive and 3 years for them to write. This book, according to the comment of analyst, is an amazing testament to the strength of the human spirit.

With series of documentary and circumstantial evidences that implicate most governments all over the world, it is safe to conclude that Satanism in government is real. Needless to point out again, Satanism has infiltrated every aspect of human life globally; including politics, cultures, traditions

And religions. Satanism have given births to monsters like Serial Ritual abuse (SRA), Satan Churches, Luciferianism, Terrorism and quite uncountable number of atrocious cult religions. It has also perverted most parts of Christianity in the world, including so-called Christian Science, Catholicism and so many other Churches that pose as Christian congregations but are in fact satanic cults in disguise.

CHAPTER SIX

<u>ORIGIN OF CULT RELIGIONS</u>

To be able to trace the origin of cult religions, tracing its source is very vital otherwise the researcher would move in a vicious circle without reaching an end. Since the only age long and reliable history book is the Bible, we have to search it and get to the bottom of the real origin of cut religions. Invariably, the research work is taking us into theology

We will start from the study of the book of Isaiah chapter 14 verses 12 to 15. The passage says, *"How art thou fallen from heaven, O Lucifer, son of the morning! how art thou cut down to the ground, which didst weaken the nations! For thou hast said in thine heart, I will ascend into heaven, I will exalt my throne above the stars of God: I will sit also upon the mount of the congregation, in the sides of the north: I will ascend above the heights of the clouds; I will be like the most High. Yet thou shalt be brought down to hell, to the sides of the pit."*

This passage of the Bible gives us an idea of who Lucifer really is and the crime he committed in heaven before he was condemned to hell. Before anyone can get the picture of what happened in heaven, these are the points to be noted first in this passage:

(I) The Most High God has His throne in heaven of heavens.

(II) There is a congregation of other beings who are angels at the lower heaven where Lucifer probably occupied a very important position.

(III) Lucifer was not satisfied with his position as an archangel. He wanted greater position like the Most High God.

(IV) He decided to promote and exalt himself, thinking of becoming like the Most High (God.)

(V) He and other angels whom he was able to influence to join in the rebellion were thrown out of heaven into hell which is far below the earth, going be other passages of the Bible like Revelation 9: 1 and 2 that describe it as bottomless pit.

The passage that best explained the struggle of Lucifer to

establish his kingdom in the kingdom of God is found in the book of Revelation chapter 12 from verses 7 to 9. It says, *"And there was war in heaven: Michael and his angels fought against the dragon; and the dragon fought and his angels, And prevailed not; neither was their place found any more in heaven. And the great dragon was cast out, that old serpent, called the Devil, and Satan, which deceiveth the whole world: he was cast out into the earth, and his angels were cast out with him."*

Also note the followings in the above passage in relation with the book of Isaiah, chapter 14 verses 12 to 15:

(I) He caused the war in heaven while trying to establish his kingdom in heaven.

(II) Lucifer had been transformed into dragon when he rebelled against God.

(III) Lucifer lost his position, his name and his real form as the son of morning but he and other fallen angels still retain their powers. So it is easy for them to transform into any creatures, including serpent which eventually deceived Eve into eating the forbidden fruits, according to the book of Genesis 3: 1 to 6.

(IV) Lucifer and the rest of the rebellious angels fell off from heaven after their defeat, making them to lose their positions in heaven. This gives them the titles of fallen angels.

(V) The fallen angels are actually thrown to hell but they still have powers to journey to and fro hell even up to the presence of God until the final judgment, according to Job 2:2. So it is easy to go to Adam Eve and tempt them to eat the forbidden fruit.

(VI) It must also be noted that Satan is still the same even though he is called by different names like Lucifer or devil or dragon.

(VII) Finally it is also instructive to note that Satan does not work alone. All the fallen angels that teamed up with him to fight Angel Michael are still working with him. They may have different names but they are commonly referred to as demons or devils or evil or unholy or foul spirits. They are all working for Satan in various ways and at various capacities. If anyone wants to imagine their number which no one can possibly guess, they can be considered to have outnumbered the numbers of stars and the people living and dead combined together.

Satan and the demons had been in existence long before existence of mankind. In fact these fallen angels know the origin of man but man did not know their origin until the most High God fully manifested Himself through Jesus Christ. Immediately after the fall of man in the Garden of Eden, man became lost and unable to trace his origin back to God Who created him. In book of Genesis chapters 6 and 7, there are events that led God to destroy the world with water. These fallen angels began to pervert God's original creation of mankind, raising children with daughters of men. These children grew into giants that brought about great wickedness with every thought of their hearts filled evil continually, according to chapter 6 verse 4 and 5. Thus God preserved Noah and his family before he eventually destroyed the world with water. Because these fallen angels cannot die, they still exist till today; making the people to do the very things that provoke God. In fact, the wickedness on earth is perfected and made sophisticated as years roll by.

As world began to increase in population, these fallen angels continue to have influence on the people up to the time of Abraham who lived with his family in his country called Ur, a city in Southern Mesopotamia of the ancient world.

The city was a prosperous centre of religion and industry. It was a kind of theocracy centered in the moon deity. It is a miracle of God's providence that Abraham resisted Ur's idolatry and set out on a journey of faith to Canaan that bless all mankind. Ur's glory was suddenly destroyed about 1900 BC. So complete was the destruction that the city was buried in oblivion until it was excavated centuries later by archaeologists.

Through Abraham, Isaac who was the father of Jacob was born. Jacob whose name was changed to Israel fathered the Israelites through whom God reveals Himself in the midst of various fallen angels that pose as gods to the people throughout the entire Old Testament until 400 years of silence, which demarcated it from the New Testament of the Bible, there are so much proves of Satanism even back then.

They came in the forms of worship of deities, sacrifices to

idols, witchcraft, sorceries and communions with these fallen angels that also manifest as various spirits; including spirits of the dead. According to the history in the Bible, God's chosen nation, Israel became vulnerable to these spirits. Various kings in Israel like Ahab who reigned in about 874 BC got so involved in Satanism that he became bad influence from one generation right after another. His wife, Jezebel who could rightly be regarded as a top Satanist in government was so involved in the worship of Baal that she had four hundred and fifty prophets of Baal and four hundred prophets of Asherah, making a total number of eight hundred and fifty Satan's priests under the play roll of the government of Israel. Elijah, the prophet demonstrated the power of the Most God when he commanded fire from heaven to consume the altar that was filled with water. He killed all the Satan's priests and got into trouble, according to 1 king 18: 19-40, 19:1-4. In spite of these subtle or violent forms, religious or spiritual, obvious or obscure ways of practicing Satanism throughout the Old Testament in the Bible, God still identify Himself as "God of Abraham, God of Isaac and God of Jacob (Israel)." The reason for adopting the name was because God made a covenant with Abraham who was childless then, saying in Genesis 12: 3 that through him all the families of the earth shall be blessed.

Idolatries in the days of the Israelites were so profound and dominant that everywhere was full of the practice of Satanism and cult religions.

According to the result of this research work, including references to the Bible and theological resource materials like New King James Version Study Bible (second edition), the angels that fell with Satan are responsible for various forms of religions, posing as both good and bad spirits. The ultimate objectives for these are to deceive and manipulate mankind. Despite the fall of man and the grand deception of Satan, mankind still longs for God; finding ways to be reconciled with Him, holding to the promises of God in the book of Isaiah in chapter 9 verses 6 and 7. The passage thus reads, *"For unto us a child is born, unto us a son is given: and the government shall be upon his shoulder: and his name shall be called Wonderful, Counsellor, The mighty God, The everlasting Father, The Prince of Peace. Of the increase of his government and peace there shall be no end, upon the throne of David, and upon his kingdom, to order it, and to establish it with judgment and with justice from henceforth even for ever. The zeal of the LORD of hosts will perform this. "*

Verse 6 of the passage speaks of the Child's humanity and given of His deity. Wonderful, Counsellor is one name, which means "Wonderful divine Counsellor" the words "Mighty God" indicates that the Lord is a powerful Warrior. "Everlasting Father" describes a King and Father who provides for and protects His people forever. Thus the word "Father" is used here of the Saviour role as an ideal King. "Prince of peace" is the climactic title. The Child is the true Prince who has the right to reign and who will usher in peace. The four double names combine aspects of Jesus' deity and humanity. Together, these four double names assert the dual nature of the Saviour. He is God become man.

In Gospel according to Saint John chapter 1 verse 1, the Bible established the deity of Jesus Christ when it says, *"in the beginning was the Word, and the Word was with God, and the Word was God. He was in the beginning with God."* In verse 14, the Bible establishes His humanity when it says, *"and the Word became flesh and dwelt among us, and we beheld his glory and truth."*

Having established the deity and the humanity of Jesus Christ, it is vital to briefly study one of His major missions in the world. This can be found also in John chapter 3 verses 16, which says, *"For God so loved the world that He gave His only begotten Son, that whosoever believes in Him should not perish but have everlasting life."*

Going by the above passage, it can be concluded that the humanity is going to perish unless there is someone to save it. So God has to send Jesus as the Saviour to humanity.

In the next verse which is 17, the Bible further says, *"For God did not send His Son into the world to condemn the world, but that the world through Him might be saved."* This means that the first coming of Jesus Christ into the world is to redeem from the fallen angels (who plan to take souls of men to hell) as many as believe in Him, saving them from the lake that burns with fire and brimstone as in Revelation 21:8.

When Jesus comes again into the world the second time, He will come to judge the world, including those who refuse

His offer of salvation, according to several passages in the Bible like 2 Timothy 4:1 which says, *"I charge thee therefore before God, and the Lord Jesus Christ, who shall judge the quick and the dead at His appearing and His kingdom..."*

There are millions of cases of people all over the world whose lives are transformed and saved from inevitable destruction that awaits humanity in hell. Even though this research work may seem academic and yet it is strictly not, it cannot ignore some outstanding testimonies that serve as case studies. This will inevitably take the works completely out of academic confinement and deal with the reality of the subject matter - Satanism and cult religion.

The testimonial case of Jeff Harshbarger is selected from among so many cases to establish some facts about Jesus and Satan. Here is the story as Jeff relates it.

"After four years in Satanism, I was miserable. I had seen everything that Satan had to offer, and still I was miserable. I decided that the only thing left to do, as a "respectable Satanist" was to kill myself. But before I even checked into the motel, I knew that something or someone might cause me to lose my nerve. For company and courage, I took along a bottle of whiskey and a bag of marijuana. I put the riffle to my head but somehow I could not pull the trigger. Disgusted with myself, I tried gain the next night. On a September night in 1981, I tried to hang myself. I put a rope over a rafter in the garage, and kicked the chair out from under me. I landed on the floor with the rope still tied to the rafter. 'What a failure,' I thought again. 'I can't even kill myself.'

"The story of my involvement in Satanism is so classic that it is almost a clinch. I was a lonely young man from a dysfunctional family. My father was an alcoholic. Things at home got worst until my mother got divorced. I had no place to belong. I was looking for people who will pay attention to me and give me acceptance. I was losing for love, and I was caught in the middle of a violent house that left me feeling hopeless and frightened. In response, I started looking into supernatural things for courage and some mystic power over my early existence. I was ripe for such an experience, and for a long time I've been interested in magic and other aspect of the paranormal. Even as a young boy, I knew that there was a spirit real, and that there had to be a way to tap to it. My first

contact with Satanism came when in 1978; snowstorm took away my hometown by surprise. I was a 17 year old high school senior, and was working in a local store during the storm. I was just beginning to wonder how I would get home that night when the store assistant manager, a young man just 18 invited me to stay at his apartment, which was just a short walk away. This young man seemed to have everything that I had ever wanted. Prestige, power - he gave every indication that he was in control of his life. That night he told me the source of his strength. I was fascinated. He showed me magic notions and occult objects which he had accumulated. Later that night, we performed a ceremony, and I gave my life to Satan.

"After I graduated from high school, my "teacher" and I moved away to attend college. The two of us attempted to begin our own satanic coven. Our coven was to consist of thirteen disciples but we were only able to recruit six, all of them are males. The six of us shared a house where we conducted what I called "freelance" satanic rituals, creating and improvising ceremonies freely. Coven activities included casting spells and desecrating Bibles and many other Christian articles that we could get our hands on. During this time, I was in contact with demons on a regular basis, though not with Satan himself.

"Eventually the frightening and distasteful parts of Satanism over shadowed the thrilling parts. I began to worry about where the coven might be headed. I knew that I could not participate in the next blood sacrifice. I knew that there were lines that I could not cross. I wanted (to opt) out. I thought, at the time, that the only thing left to do was to kill myself. To my dismay, I failed. Now I know that only Divine intervention could have saved me from both gun and the noose.

"After returning home, I tried to drink myself into the oblivion, but found that the taste of beer turned my stomach. So instead I lit a cigarette to calm my nerves but it burned my lips! So finally, I, the Satanist priest in the making went to my room, lay in my bed and began to cry. I will never forget in my life what happened next.

"It was late at night. The rest of the coven was out partying so the house was empty. Out of the silence, I heard a voice *from behind my bed that said, 'Get out!' I stopped crying and look round the room, expecting the presence of a demon. The voice moved to the feet of my bed and said again, 'GET OUT!' I remember being so shaken by the command that I immediately obeyed. I crawled out of the nearest window in my bedroom and into the drive way and into the presence of God. My feet went weak and I fell on my face, there was no mistaking who this was. Looking up at the sky, I pleaded, 'Jesus, just make my life, ok.'*

"I have come a long way from those days in the Satanism. I still believe in a spiritual realm. I believe in a spiritual realm and I believe in both demons and angels, evil and good. I have simply traded darkness for light. The Lord has helped me through complete recovery. I have been married now for 15 years. My wife Liz and I live in Bonita Springs, Florida. With God's help I have earned master's degree in counselling and have launched REFUGE ministries. Together, we instruct others about the dangers of occult and how to help someone through deliverance."

There is another case of a woman who is now a Christian. In her story written in a book titled, "From Satan To Christ," she revealed the secrets of Satanists that laid bare as the depraved leaders are identified and their loathsome cult is exposed with sensational photographic evidence of the occult underworld. This woman who was born into an English 'Shire family' describes in her story what ostensibly appeared to be witchcraft coven which slowly revealed itself to be a Satanist cult that is involved in every profanity and evil act imaginable - devil worship, live sacrifice, demon raising, blood rituals, death curses, black masses and host of evils like that came up in the cause of this research work. The frightening facts behind some of today's covens are best revealed by someone who was inside the cult.

With the cases of this woman and Jeff Harshbarger, it must be noted that the longer a person stays in Satanism, the more evil or deadly he or she becomes. A lot of people like Jeff are dabblers who dabble into Satanism either out of curiosity or ignorance or desire to possess supernatural powers.

Polls in the UK as at compiling the results of this research works indicate that those who subscribe to occult and "alternative" belief system, including witchcraft and Satanism now by far outnumber Christians in Great Britain. This explains why so many Christian ministries are going into oblivion.

Cult religions all over the world are getting more rampant, taking so many forms that it will take eternity to study each of them. With advanced technologies, sophisticated means of information, education and entertainments and with their infiltrations into politics, Satanism and cult religions all over world are growing gigantically monstrous. Cult religions are taking far more sophisticated forms than it used to be few years ago. They have infiltrated into the lifestyles, norms, cultures of the people and even their constitutions. The acts that constitute anti-social ways of life in the past had become part of the law with sanctions against anyone that discriminate against those who practice them. These, unknown to most people, are acts of Satanism.

The act of Satanism and practice of cult religions are very broad and complicated, if not confusing. For the sake simplicity, the next chapters will address Satanism in the modern and information age. Through this and with references to the results of research works of others, it would be proven that Satanism is well established in technologies, entertainment, cultures and other aspects of human life.

CHAPTER SEVEN

<u>SATANISM IN MODERN AND INFORMATION AGE</u>

Carlo Climatic of Regina Apostolorum Pontifical university, who specializes in the dangers posed to young people by Satanism says that it has never been easier to sell your soul to the devil. According to him, the internet makes it a doddle to find information about Satanism. In just a few minutes, you can contact Satanist groups and research cultism. In the good old days, the Church could stop the flow of such information (or contact with Satanist group) by arranging book burnings in the public place (as in the case in the book of Acts of Apostles chapter 19 verse 19). But with information technology and legislation, this is impossible.

As a result of technology in the information age, dealing with shed loads of demons which have come flooding from the kingdom of darkness as a result of people finding out Satanism and cult religions, it is becoming more and more difficult to combat them even with lots of Christian books and publications that expose them. The deception in the technology of the internet for instance is overwhelming, making it hard if not impossible for most people to differentiate truths from lies. A person who is filled with lies on the internet may see himself to be full of knowledge without knowing that he has actually become a Satanist or Satanic tool of manipulation. Series of convincing articles and satanic teachings fill the world like ocean with hardly any ground for truth to stand upon. Sadly enough, the truth had become so scare to get that even the Church, which was once known to be truthful is deceived into believing lies. It is of little wonder that Jesus asks in Luke 18: 8 that if He comes back, would He find faith on earth.

With Satanism dominating technology in this information age, there is hardly truth anywhere in the whole world except the word of God - The Bible. Even then, so many people make the Bible appears like ordinary book. Many Satanists, including the atheists try to flaw and even condemn it but God keeps proving it to people that the Word of God is life.

Remember that Satanism is a stronghold in the world.

From generations to generations, Satanism and cult religions grow like cancer all over the world.

Mark Lallanilla reported on 1st August 2013 that there was a mysterious pentagram on Google maps. The strange pentagram, etched into the Earth's surface in a remote corner of Kazakhstan. He said, *"conspiracy theorists, start your engines."*

According to this report, archaeologists has revealed the source of the mysterious structures, saying that the five-pointed star surrounded by a circle shows up vividly with almost no other signs of human habitations in the area. The closest settlement is the city of Lisakovsk, about 12 miles (20km) to the east.

The region surrounding Lisakovsk is riddled with ancient archaeological ruins. Bronze Age settlements, cemeteries and burial grounds - many of which are yet to be explored. What is this bizarre symbol, which measure roughly 1,200 feet (366 meters) in diameter doing on the side of a desolate lake in northern Kazakhstan? Many online comments linked the site with devil worship, nefarious religious sects or denizens of the underworld.

Upon zooming into the center of the pentagram, viewer will see two places highlighted by previous visitors to Google maps. One spot is called Adam, the other, Lucifer.

The Kazakh pentagram certainly is not the first odd discovery gleaned from Google maps, according to Marc's report. This proves to everybody in the world that Satanism is almost as old as the earth itself.

The author of this book also wrote a another book with the title: "The Beast In All Nations Of The World" where he presents and paints the Biblical pictures of the wars in heaven and on earth in a drama form. The book also reveals how ancient practices of Satanism have been transformed into sophisticated ways of life and cult religions in the present technology and information age.

There are a few attributes of Satanism in the modern day which differ from the ancient practices although they still share the same characteristics.

One of the attributes is the sophistication of Satanism in the modern days. Someone remarked that Satan masterminds technology. While this remark may sound controversial, it is instructive to note that Satanists make best use of technology to spread Satanism all over the world. So many parents who allow their children to parent themselves have given room for Satanism to creep into their homes through the internet, television and other means of entertainment, information and education. Children know a lot about their world much more than their parents. Because the world is full of lies and deceptions, they never know the truth without the help of those who actually know the truth. In fact, they have been programmed by the things they can perceive with their human sense to argue with the truth.

Satanism has many ways of making people hide their true colour or identity. That is the reason a person who seems like a good Christian may turn out to be a Satanist if the truth about him or her is revealed .

Secondly, modern Satanists have many sophisticated ways of getting hold of their members. Some new converts in Satanism do not need to leave their rooms to get connected with other Satanists. The numbers of satanic web sites and materials all over the world have by far outnumbered that of the Gospel. With the use of these web sites and materials, it is a lot easy to have more and more converts in satanic groups.

The third attribute in modern Satanism is the various shapes it has taken. A satanic group can pose as a Christian Church. Before the new converts of the "Christian Church" know that they are involved in Satanism, they would have gone deep side - perhaps up to the point of making blood sacrifice. There is a case study of a Christian woman who went to visit one of her relations in a small town in Africa. When it was Sunday, she decided to go to the nearest Church, which unknown to her practiced Satanism. Because she is a Christian who is used to Christian pattern of worship, she was able to note that she was in a satanic gathering, which posed as Christian congregation. Of course, she sneaked out of the Church. She decided that she would rather stay at home and worship God with one or two other Christians than to join any congregation she is not familiar with.

Another attributes of modern day Satanism is materialism. Satanists use materialism to lure people into Satanism. As most people all over the world are materialistic, they are vulnerable. They can be enticed either to get involved in Satanism or become victims of cult religions.

The revelation of Samuel Butler indicates that satanic cults build large underground bunkers and a very luxurious compound but the underground is where the evil deeds are done like sacrificing human beings.

Vigilant Citizen reported on January 3rd, 2012 of a case of Lady Gaga who was accused of performing satanic rituals in a hotel room.

According to the staff of London's Intercontinental Hotel, Lady Gaga left her room's bath filled with blood. Her room house keeper stated that Gaga was *"bathing in blood as part of a satanic ritual."*

Another article from the Independent Newspapers confirmed that Lady Gaga left large amount of blood in a hotel bath. It says, *"the eccentric singer reportedly shocked staff when she checked out of London's lavish Intercontinental Hotel last summer and they discovered a pool of red liquid in the tub, which the housekeeper confirmed was blood. She said the pop super star was 'bathing in blood as part of a satanic ritual.' An insider said, 'all of the hotel's staffs are convinced she was bathing in it (the blood).'* The report further indicated that it was not the first time Lady Gaga has been accused of unusual behaviour in hotels.

Materialism, which may include wealth, fame power or connections is a very strong satanic tool to lure people into Satanism and cult religions as in the case of Jeff Harshbarger.

In addition to using mouth-watering materialism to package evil with glamourous wrappers, tools of media and entertainments that showcase Satanism are also used. Anyone who takes the bait of materialism would need a major miracle before getting off the hook. The case of Michael Jackson who was both a participant and victim of Satanism and cult religions is a classic example. His case will give a vivid picture of how Satanists like the illuminati uses music and other means of entertainments to brainwash people, spreading Satanism through coded messages.

Michael Jackson was born in August 29, 1958 in Gary, Indiana. He was a singer and a songwriter. His award winning career as the king of pop transformed the face of pop music and popular culture. He died unexpectedly on June 25, 2009.

The circumstances surrounding his death and his foreknowledge about his death which he shared with his ex-wife, Liza Marie Presley, the daughter of Elvis Presley are noteworthy.

Like her father, like ex-husband, Lisa said she was horrified by parallels between Michael Jackson and Elvis Presley's deaths. She poured out her heart about her twenty-month marriage to Michael Jackson and recounted the conversation they had 14 years before his death.

When Liza was asked what she has got to say about her twenty-month marriage with him, she said, *"to say the least, I am still in shock. I can still imagine him staring at me very intensely and he started with an almost calm certainty. He said, 'I am afraid that I am going to end up like Elvis the way he died.'"*

Elvis Presley was just 42 when he died at his Memphis mansion. The cause of his death was said to be cardiac arrest but it was clear that his years of pill popping had contributed.

Liza was his young daughter then and now she was forced to confront exact scenario once again as she watched reports of another failed superstar, Michael Jackson, with a penchant for painkillers deed of cardiac arrest. It all reminded her of that long ago talk she had with Michael Jackson.

The story which Satanists, particularly the Illuminati would not want anybody to hear about the death of Michael Jackson has to do with his lifelong affiliation with them. The affiliation eventually terminated his life when he attempted to expose them through hidden messages in his songs like "Dangerous," "Remember the time," "Keep the Faith" and "Invisible", which was his final studio album before his death.

Since in his childhood days in the Jackson Five, Michael was taught the secrets of a group of top Satanists known as Illuminati. This Satanist group had been in the practice of recruiting popular performers, making them to insert subliminal and mind control messages in their songs.

After achieving the rank sof king of pop, Michael Jackson began to realize the danger the Illuminati presented to mankind. He approached the CIA, offering to spill the secrets in exchange for protection. He probably did not understand that the Illuminati is well represented in the CIA at every level though he knew he could not speak out directly against the monstrous Satanists. After hiding his messages in some songs, Michael Jackson sensed his days were numbered. Fearing the Illuminati could shoot him down, he asked the CIA in the album which was included in the Free Will, *"Will You Be There?"*

The Illuminati attempted to discredit him through child molestation charges. When they failed, they got rid of him.

With Michael Jackson out of the way, the Illuminati plans to brainwash the people through entertainment coalition with Kanye West, Drake, Jay Z, Rihanna, Ice Cube, Lady Gaga, Britney Spears and a host of others

There are also overwhelming evidence that prove that these Satanists also introduce Satanism to children through computer games and cartoons. A good example of these cartoons is titled: Lou Minatic. With subliminally destructive messages embedded in movies, music, computer games and cartoons, Satanism had been spreading like wild fire that is ready to consume the entire world.

The effects of satanic messages can easily be observed through shared wrong values on social media and online forums. It is shocking to note the number of people who are ignorantly involved in Satanism and cult religions due to the glamour that is associated with this technique. Different categories of people, particularly youths often pick wrong persons as their heroes or role models in movies or musicals. This often influences them to follow their ways of life. If these role models are involved in Satanism or cult religions, it is instructive to note their fans will naturally get involved in them either in conscious or unconscious manners.

Although modern day practice of Satanism is much more effective in the influence, involvements, spread of atrocities and initiations of members than in the ancient day practice of cult religions through means of technology but they both have a lot in common.

Some of the things that are common to them is sacrifices of both human lives and animals. With few cases that have been treated so far, it is instructive to note that when a person dabbles into Satanism, he or she first starts off by signing a deal with Satan through cutting his finger or getting a bit of his blood to give his soul to him, as pointed out earlier. He graduates from there into using animal sacrifices. With time, he is mandated to bring a person for sacrifice. The moment he begins to get involved in human sacrifices, he becomes a "clean-cut Satanist." Such Satanists, according to Samuel Butler, are the ones to watch out for. They are so inhuman that they can use even their own children as sacrifices.

The other things that are common to modern and ancient days practice of Satanism are the use of lies, deceptions, fear, hypnotism and hypocrisy to either ensnare dabblers or enslave members of satanic group who may be planning to opt out.

In the findings of Gene and Earline Moody, written in form of teachings titled: "Deliverance Manual" confirms the followings:

"There is astonishing, hideous rise of devil worship, Satanism, and witchcraft among the youths. You will be shaken, startles and disgusted. Witchcraft is on the rise throughout the world.

"You especially need to learn about witchcraft and the New Age Movement. There are perhaps five to seven millions active witches in America today and another five millions or so persons who have studied or dabbled in witchcraft, which is a very small branch of Satanism in its entirety.

"(Satanist's) plan promotes New Age Movement and (cult) religions, rituals, idolatry, belief in reincarnation, fantasy books and games, white magic, black magic, sorcery, shamanism, polytheism, occult symbols, objects and idols, psychology, UFO's and extra terrestrials, witchcraft and Satan worship, astrology and horoscope, tarot card reading, Oui ja boards, palm readings, fire-walking, seances, mediums, spirit channeling, holistic medicine, physical tests and sports, guided imagery and visualization.

"Basically these are occultic rituals, beliefs, practices, artifacts and objects including butchery, violence and sex. Shows are full of sexual license, magic, sorcery, and satanic violence and evil...

'Many other doctrines, rituals, practices and symbols have been received from the past by the New Age Movement.

There is a gigantic conspiracy underway. Billions will join the Jesus-hating forces of the New Age Beast.

"The word occult simply means hidden or concealed, kept from views. Here is just a partial list of ancient satanic teachings, practices and symbols now in vogue and being pushed on the children and teens: Colour therapy, heavy metal music, unisex dress, sadism, sorcery, incests and immorality, hypnotism, New Age mood music, palmistry, rebellion, astral travel (or projection),mystery teachings, ESP (Psychic Powers), God as mother (nature instead of Almighty God or Father as in the Bible), astrology, nature worship, rhythmic breathing, visualization, psychedelic drugs, sodomy, feminism, necromancy, dragons, pyramids, chanting, yoga, demonic music, fortune telling, levitation, self-love, fire-walking, body tattoos, numerology, pedophilia, mental images; the unicorn, Pegasus and other magical beasts; communication with the dead; meditation (other than on God's word the Bible); satanic symbols (like pentagram, triangle, circle and a host of others.)

"Practice of dealing with evil spirits, use of sorcery or magic, to whisper a spell, enchant or magic are also examples of practice of Satanism (and cult religions). Enchantment (song spell or Augur) - act of influencing by charms and incantations, practice of magical arts, hypnosis, spell casting, soothsayer and sorcerer are all acts of sorcery or witchcraft. (Note that these are all ancient practices that are now modernized. The songs that cast spells on people are evident in modern day musical concert and albums where the witch or sorcerer that posses as music superstar holds the audience spell bound. Case study of Lady Gaga and host of others can be considered as the modern day spell castings.)

"Every adult, especially Christians have to learn to understand the fact that Satan wants to teach and get their children involved in Satanism (and cult religions). He wants to make them knowledgeable in the occult teachings of the New Age which is gaining lots of ground in the world. Parents, grandparents, educators and pastors need to discern the spirit of the time. They need to walk in the light of the word of God before they can repel the gross darkness in the world. This will take a well-informed stand for God's truth

in the modern days."

The picture of the condition of the world is depicted in the book of Revelation 12:12 which says, *"Therefore rejoice, you heavens, and you that dwell in them. Woe to the inhabiters of the earth and of the sea! for the devil is come down unto you, having great wrath, because he knows that he hath but a short time."*

The story which may also illustrate the condition of the world is titled: The Game Of Life. It goes thus:

There are two opposing teams who are involved in the game of life in a stadium called The World. The two teams are called The Flesh and The Spirit. This game demands that each team must convert the players in the opposing team to their sides. The Flesh team is made up of professional foul players that are characterized by the spirits of Adultery, Fornication, Uncleanness, Lewdness, idolatry, Sorcery, Hatred, Contentions, Jealousies, Wrath, Selfish-Ambitions, Dissensions, Heresies, Envy, Murders, Drunkenness, Revelries and many others that are opposed to the rules of the game of life called The Bible. (Galatians 5:19-21).

The players in The Spirit team are descent people who play by the rules of the game because they are characterized by fruits of the Holy Spirit called Love, Joy, Peace, Long-suffering, kindness, Goodness, Faithfulness, Gentleness and Self-Control. (Galatians 5:22-23). The result of the game will determine the eternal destinations of all the players, both in The Flesh and The Spirit teams. Whoever plays by the rules of the game will end up getting a mansion in the place of eternal bliss called Heaven but whosoever does not play by the rules will end up in a lake that burns with fire and brimstone called Hell. (Revelation 21:7-8).

In order to ensure that the players in The Spirit team plays by the rules of the game, the coach called Jesus Christ gives the members a Guardian called Holy spirit who directs them in the way to play. The coach of The Flesh team called Satan or devil, however, ensures that members of his team do not play by the rules by giving them so many guardians called Unholy Spirits or devils.

Satan not only deceives and manipulates the players in The Flesh team with the use of things they can perceive with their human senses, he also uses them to deceive everybody in the stadium, teaching them how to violate the rules and how to deceive opponent players. (2 Timothy 3:13).

While players in The Flesh team are constantly seeking to win people in the stadium to their side, strange enough, most of the players in The Spirit team are doing little or nothing about gaining people to their sides. Consequently, the stadium becomes filled with corrupt players.

With the audiences in Heaven and Hell, which are quite invisible to the people at the stadium, there is always joy on the side of The Flesh team whenever a player in The Spirit team falls into their hands. Even then, there is always also joy in Heaven if a player in The Flesh team is converted to The Spirit team (Luke 15:7).

The above story further depicts the fact that any time the dark side of supernatural world is presented as a harmless or even imaginary thing to everybody, especially children, the people become very curious or even eager for the power. Of course, this will pose the danger of vulnerabilities. With their vulnerabilities or curiosities, it becomes very easy to lure them into Satanism and cult religions until it is too late if not outrightly impossible to rescue them.

In a culture with an obvious trend towards witchcraft and New Age ideology, everybody needs to consider the effects that these ideas may have on young and impressionable minds. Christian parents, teachers, pastors and counter-cult ministry workers need to note that children tend to be less aggressive if they are raised in a warm and loving atmosphere. Parents who tend to be cold and stand-offish or rejecting with children will produce more hostile offsprings. In the United States, television has become the major form of relaxation after a hard day at the office. But, Americans are being fooled! What they perceive as relaxation is actually stimulating some very unfavourable feelings with visible consequences.

By the age of two or three, most children regularly watch 26-33 hours of television each week, going by research works. 98 percent of all households have at least TV turned on an average of 6 hours per day. In an average evening of television viewing, deadly weapons appear about nine times per hour. 75 percent act of all prime-time network drama contains some act of physical, mental, or verbal violence. 40

percent of all prime TV shows are considered to be very high in violence.

The average child has watched the violent destructions of more than 13,000 persons on TV by time he is fifteen. (Note: this violence is similar to the ancient days of entertainment like the gladiators in the ancient Rome.) At current notes, the average American will view 45,000 murders or attempted murders on television by the age of 21. 78 percent of parents have used the television as a baby sitter at one time or the other. By the time of high School graduation, most children have spent about 11,000 hours in school, but more than 22,000 hours in front of the TV.

On the average, most American children see 250 episodes of war cartoons and 800 advertisements for war toys per year. War cartoons, complete with their own line of war toys continue to appear with each new season. War cartoons average approximately 80 violent acts per hour with an attempted murder every two minutes. These programmes show characters that enjoy repeated attempts to kill each other. Usually the character who is considered good is never killed. Whether prime-time TV, Saturday morning and after school cartoons and shows, big screen novels, nowhere can safely be found for the children.

The realism of movies and TV is demonic free fire bottle zone and the children are hapless targets. Shows like medium, Supernatural, charmed, Buffy - The Vampire Slayer, and Sabrina - The Teenage Witch and so many others that are springing up everyday blatantly promote and glamourized and modernized witchcraft.

Imagine (just like the ancient day barbarism) how tens of thousands of scenes of New Age, barbarism (in modernized forms), butchery, violence, sex, sorcery, mythical gods and goddesses, space aliens, creatures and occultism are seen by the average child during say, the first 12 years of life alone, and you begin to realize the gravity and seriousness of what is happening to the kids.

There is a belief that the kid's thoughts create reality for them. Images are printed upon subconscious mind. The Third Eye, All Seeing Eye or Mind's Eye are all occult. Ascended Masters are supposed to be highly evolved spirit-being (actually fallen angels) who makes decisions concerning the lives of New Ages. These stories prepare children to seek after the secret things of Satan.

Satanism is obviously getting more and more sophisticated and complicated, going by this and other findings of researchers. Hence it is instructive to note that all aspects of life are infiltrated with Satanism and cult religions.

CHAPTER EIGHT

<u>SEX TOOLS OF GROSS DARKNESS</u>

In Isaiah 60:2, the Bible says, *"For behold, the darkness shall cover the earth, And deep darkness the people; But the Lord will arise over you, And His glory shall be seen upon you."*

Darkness is absence of light just as evil is the absence of God's presence. The world was without light when it was created by God, according to Genesis 1:2, which means it is without God's presence. When God's presence manifested through His Word, light came. The light makes the world to look good, going by verses 3 and 4. As the world begins to advance in age after creation of man, the presence of God begins to reduce, making darkness to return into the world through the manifestations of the prince of darkness who took over the rulership from Adam. It became so full of evil that the Bible says in Genesis 6:5-6, *"Then the Lord saw that the wickedness of man was great in the earth, and that every intent of the thoughts of his (man's) was only evil continually. And the Lord was sorry that He had made man on the earth, and He was grieved in this heart."*

If the story of "Game Of Life" is related with the issue of gross darkness in the world, it would be noted that the players in The Flesh team are carnal people who have no faintest idea of what they are doing or what is going on the realm of the spirit or the eternal death that awaits them in hell. They are easily be used, manipulated and misled just as a blind man can be misled.

This world where all humans are key players in the game of life is full darkness throughout history of man up till now. In fact the prince of darkness - Satan relentlessly spreads darkness on the face of the earth, influencing man to enjoy darkness much more than light because he knows he has only short time before he his bound to the lake of fire, going by the passage in Revelation 12:12. Thus Jesus said in John 3:19, *"And this is the condemnation, that light is come into the world, and men loved darkness rather than light, because their deeds were evil."*

Ironically the prince of darkness was once the son of morning when he was in the presence of God, according to Isaiah 14:12. After he was thrown out of the presence of God and cast into the world, he became evil one that is full of darkness. He is the prince of darkness that spreads darkness over all nations through deception and lies. He uses other fallen angels that are also full of darkness to accomplish his deadly missions which, according to John 10:10, are to steal the souls of men by enticing them to defy God, kill them spiritually by disconnecting them from source of light of men - Jesus Christ (John 1:4) and then destroys them in the lake that burns with fire and brimstone (Revelation 21:8).

In Revelation 12:7-9, the Bible gives graphic picture of how the personality of son of morning became the prince of darkness, listing his characteristics. The Bible also explains how he spreads darkness all over the world in Isaiah 14:12-21.

Part of the things that made the prince of darkness to lose his position in the kingdom of God are what he introduces into the world. These things which have increased over the years are so much, so demonic, so sophisticated, so subtle and at times so obscure that it will require the thorough study of the Bible and series of observations of the operations of the devils before anyone can detect them. They are responsible or used to spread darkness all over the world. They are everywhere in the world and in all walks of life such as in politics, economics, education, religions and so many other areas. These things may not be necessarily spiritual but they are ideal tools of demons. Some of these things are found in Galatian 5:19-21, which says, *"Now the works of the flesh are manifest, which are these; Adultery, fornication, uncleanness, lasciviousness, Idolatry, witchcraft, hatred, variance, emulations, wrath, strife, seditions, heresies, Envyings, murders, drunkenness, revellings, and such like: of the which I tell you before, as I have also told you in time past, that they which do such things shall not inherit the kingdom of God."*

The lists of these things above are growing by the day. The devils make use of them to bring about gross darkness upon the face of the earth. Hence, he makes people engage in the things which will defy God and deny them access to heaven.

These eternally deadly things are painted into fanciful and fashionable ways of life. No doubt, the devils make it a pleasurable thing to be engaged in the kind of rebellion that made him and other fallen angels lose the kingdom of God.

Because man is still in the flesh, one of the major tools to spread darkness is sex. This tool needs to be studied critically in line with what is observed in the world.

Sexually Transmitted Diseases (STD) operates very much like Sexually Transmitted Darkness. The first two sins on the list of lust of the flesh as recorded in the book of Galatians chapter 5 verses 19 to 21 are sexual immoralities called adultery and fornication. The reason they are the first is that it is the easiest way of spreading darkness, going by the results of various research works. There is a case study in the Bible that establishes this fact in Genesis chapter 6 verses 1 to 5.

The study of the above passage indicates that when the devil took over the world, he became the god of this world. The fallen angels who were once called sons of God but now called the devils or demons went ahead to pervert mankind by having sex with beautiful daughters of men. These beautiful women produced children of the fallen angels in the world. The consequence of that was to have partly human and partly demon giants who were so wicked that God decided to destroy human beings, preserving His original human creation through Noah and the pairs of each animal that could not survive inside water.

Since the devil succeeded in spreading darkness throughout the world through sex, provoking God to destroy it, it follows therefore that sexual immoralities are part of the major tools of darkness. The tools of sexual immoralities are designed in a number of ways but in whichever way or form each of them comes, it must be considered demonic. The tools vary from one to another, from one generation to another, from one community to another and from one nation to another. Invariably, all are from the same source - the prince of darkness, Satan.

Although the list of the tools cannot be exhausted but the ones that are common need to be treated

Sex Appeal Tools

Some people are naturally good looking even though

most of them cannot handle the challenges that go along with good looks. Some people who are not attractive can be made attractive or, to use the secular terms, "sexy". The prince of darkness usually recruits people with sex appeal as members of his flesh team either with their knowledge or not. Some who are not even attractive can be made to serve the same purpose of spreading darkness through sex as long as they made themselves available.

Having enlisted people as sex tools, the prince of darkness influences them to consciously or unconsciously enter a covenant with him by having sex with people who are not their spouses or who possessed any type of demon, usually in the class of principalities. The good look of a person is a very ideal sex tool to appeal to others to have sex with him or her. The real life story of the snake demon that turned itself into a beautiful lady in Nigeria is a classic example of how far the devils can go to destroy mankind or to spread darkness.

The fact in this case is that a woman was hard pressed while travelling with others passengers in a bus. The driver parked the bus by the road side and allowed her to go inside the nearby bush and ease herself. As soon as she stooped to ease herself, she saw a python turning into a beautiful young lady. The snake woman walked to the side of the road where other passengers saw a man driving a jeep, picking her up before the woman returned to the bus.

Using this case study, it is easy to imagine what can happen to the man that picked the snake demon up in his jeep. The man may take her to the hotel where he could be struck dead if she turned back into a snake. Other possibility is that she may allow him to have sex with her just as the story in Genesis 6:1-5 and then part ways, allowing him to spread the demonic contact through sex with other ladies who may also spread it to other people. The Bible passage says, *"And it came to pass, when men began to multiply on the face of the earth, and daughters were born unto them, That the sons of God saw the daughters of men that they were fair; and they took them wives of all which they chose. And the LORD said, My spirit shall not always strive with man, for that he also is flesh: yet his days shall be an hundred and twenty years. There were giants in the earth in those days; and also after that, when the sons of God came in unto the daughters of men, and they bare children to them, the same became mighty men which were of old, men of renown. And GOD saw that the wickedness of man was great in the earth, and that every imagination of the thoughts of his heart was only evil continually."*

The implication of having sex with a demon that posed as a beautiful lady is to make the man a potential vessel to destroy others or to spread darkness through sex.

As pointed out, what is applicable in Sexually Transmitted Diseases (STD) is also applicable to Sexually Transmitted Darkness (STD) or Sexually Transmitted Destruction (STD) or Sexually Transmitted Death (STD). In other words all the women that have sex with the man after meeting with the snake demon will be infected with STD. All the men that have sex with all the women, including their husbands after meeting with the man that met with the snake demon will be infected with STD. This implies that the spread of STD is to have infected people who are dying or going straight to hell unless they turn their lives completely over to Jesus Christ for deliverance.

The author came across the case of a man who was once possessed with something like snake demon. He told him he constantly had sex with the snake in the dream. He did not know how he got possessed but he knew it was through one of his numerous bed mates. After turning his life over to Christ, Jesus went to him in the dream and pull out a very big snake from his body. He became completely delivered.

Although some cases are much more complicated than the other but no case is hopeless as long as the victim of the prince of darkness is ready to surrender his or her life completely to Jesus Christ.

Sex is so appealing that everybody, including matured Christians can be tempted or vulnerable. That is the reason the Bible says in 1 Corinthians 6: 18, *"Flee fornication. Every sin that a man does is without the body; but he that commits fornication sins against his own body."*

The passage is saying in other words that sexual immorality is not what everyone should just pray against but to run away from as fast he or she can, including closing the gateway of the eyes or turning the eyes away from it so that it does not tempt or appeal to him or her. The reason, according to that passage, is that sexual immorality gives room for powerful demons to possess the bodies of the adulterers and fornicators. Sex is only good if it is done within the confine of marriage. It is a holy covenant between the wife and the husband. It is also a very demonic covenant if it is enjoyed outside the confine of marriage.

While trying to sexually appeal to others, so many; especially women consciously or unconsciously apply demonic cosmetic items on their bodies such as the perfume of Lady Gaga and a whole lot of other items that are dedicated to the devils. Such cosmetics or items are actually meant to attract people to those who apply them on their bodies. This explains the reason so many people cannot do without make-ups or perfumes. Most, if not all these items are designed to lure people into sexual immoralities.

Another thing that serves as sex appeal tool is the clothing, most especially the ones that reveal the body. Modern fashions have no respect for morals or traditional values, which is typical of demonic items. The design of most of the closings nowadays are actually demon inspired with the principal aim of making people as young as ten years sexually promiscuous. There are some cloth designs that are meant for adults even by secular world about twenty years ago but through advertisements; they are now considered for girls as young as seven years old.

According to the report by Mibba Creative Writing, in 2013, Abercrombie & Fitch released a new line of sexually suggestive thong underwear to young girls. In a statement to ABC News, A&F stated that the underwear was meant to be *"light hearted and cute."* The company also stated that the product was created for girls that were 10 and over, even though it was found in the Abercrombie kids line for girls aged 7 -14.

"That makes me angry," Kevin Delacruz said, *"Everyone is exposed to sex through media at some point in their lives, but exposing someone so young can negatively influence their thinking and how they look at themselves and others."*

"Clothing companies," Mibba Creative Writing stated, *"such as A&F, Hollister and American Apparel have been pushing boundaries and using sex to sell their clothing for*

many years. Other product companies have started taking advantage of this as well."

One of the major things that accounted for high rate of rape all over the world is the kind of clothing which females are influenced to wear either through advertisements or music or movie stars. The kind of clothing anyone puts on tells others the kind of spirits that controls or inspires him or her. It is the spirit that will attract people to have a taste of his or her juice, which is actually meant to be enjoyed within the confine of marriage.

Tools Of Sodomy

An organization called Rings of Equality claims to be an outlet for inspirational and thought-provoking gay relationship stories and stories of gay marriage. Their goal, according to their claim, is to promote cultural acceptance and positive change for same-sex couples. They have the belief that further acceptance of gay relationships will only strengthen their society. They want to work with people to find numerous same-sex marriage stories that are interesting and moving to share with their visitors, both supporters and opponents of gay marriage.

This organization, according to the result of this research work into gross darkness is a group of sodomites that use the tools of sodomy to spread darkness. There are so many of them like that all over the world, seeking sympathy and relevance among the people.

Sodomites who consciously or unconsciously practice Satanism or cult religions had been existing at least as long as the days of Sodom and Gomorrah in Genesis 14:8-11 and their atrocities rage from homosexuality, lesbianism, paedophilia, practices of sex with animals and dead people.

The Sodomites often use their freedom as a license and the law as tools to spread darkness. They do not limit these atrocities to themselves. They also try to use the law to get supports or sympathies of others in their atrocities. A case study on that is the report by Zack Ford in 2013 about a Colorado Judge who said a Christian Baker that refused wedding Cake to same-sex couples broke the law. What is particularly intriguing about this case was that the State does not recognize same-sex marriage at that time which gave the Christian baker the discretion to refuse or accept to bake the cake but the Administrative law judge Robert Spencer ruled against Jack Phillips, the owner of the bakery on the ground that the religious freedom did not justify Phillips' violation of Colorado's nondiscrimination law protecting sexual orientation. The judge is not persuaded by the Respondent's argument that they need not be compelled to recognize same-sex marriage, especially when Colorado does not do so.

The case typically illustrates how far Sodomites are ready to advance their atrocities, using the law, media, publications and means of entertainment and education to spread their activities that are condemned by God.

In 1 Corinthians 6:9-10 the Bible says, *"Know you not that the unrighteous shall not inherit the kingdom of God? Be not deceived: neither fornicators, nor idolaters, nor adulterers, nor effeminate, nor ABUSERS OF THEMSELVES WITH MANKIND, Nor thieves, nor covetous, nor drunkards, nor revilers, nor extortioners, shall inherit the kingdom of God."*

The above passage makes it clear that sodomy is not a modern day act but an age old atrocity. Sodomy can thus be literarily and biblically defined as any of various forms of sexual intercourse held to be obnoxious or unnatural or abnormal; including anal intercourse or bestiality. In physiology, it is anal intercourse committed by a man or a woman. It is also oral copulation with a member of opposite sex. Sodomy laws in many countries criminalize not only the behaviours, but other disfavoured sexual activities as well. In the Western World, however, many of these laws have been overturned or are not routinely enforced.

In the various criminal codes of the U. S, the term "Sodomy" has generally been replaced by the term Deviant Sexual Intercourse. These sodomy laws have been challenged and have sometimes be found unconstitutional or have been replaced with different legislation.

In some countries like Zimbabwe, the Sodomy Law is effective; going by the report by Fungai Lupande of The Herald. In the report: "Sodomy Councilor At it Again," it was stated that councilor Sydney Chirombe was in court to answer to a Sodomy charge for the second time in 2014 after he was arrested in Willowrale industrial area while allegedly having sex with another man in a car.

While some countries frown at Sodomy because it was unnatural sexual behaviour, some like America embrace it and consider it a sexual orientation which needs to be tolerated. In fact, in such countries that allow homosexual, lesbianism and sodomy bahaviours; the law makes it an offence to discriminate against those who practice them as in the case of Jack Philips that refused to bake wedding cake for same-sex couple. Using the law as a tool, the prince of darkness sexually transmits darkness and destruction through sodomy. The same spirit that possesses a person who is sexually involved with another person who is of the same sex is the one that inspires others to persecute anyone who goes against them like the case of Jack Phillips. The same spirit is also the one that possesses a person who has sex with a beast or a dead person.

<u>Pornographic Tools</u>

This is another easy way to spread darkness. According to Wikipedia definition of pornography, it is the explicit portrayal of sexual subject matter for the purpose of sexual arousal. It may be presented in a variety of media, including books, magazines, postcards, photographs, sculptures, drawings, paintings, animations, sound recordings, film, videos and video games.

Although the victim of prince of darkness may not necessarily get involved in sex at the time pornographic tool is used but a stage is set for the demon to operate through the victim. More obviously, this tool can be used to make a person exhibits the lust of flesh which the Bible calls lasciviousness or lewdness in Galatians 5:19.

Using the eyes majorly as a gateway to the life or soul of victim, darkness can infiltrate into a man or woman and then makes it easy for demons to operate. One pornographic item is all a demon requires before setting stage for others to gain access into the life or soul. With the use of these items, a naturally gentle person can turn into a rapist overnight if he or she is not satisfied with masturbation. Once a person is involved in pornography, to let it go will take a miracle.

One terrible thing about pornographic tools is that they can be used as a weapon against anyone, no matter whom the person is - be it a Christian or not, disciplined or not, married or not. The prince of darkness knows how effective this tool can be if it is well used. Hence, he introduced pornography into nearly everything that can be viewed with the eyes; including advertisements, internet, movies, magazines, photography, books, television and other things.

Unlike other items that can be consumed through the use of the mouth or body such as food; cloths and perfume; pornographic items do not need to be dedicated to the prince of darkness or the devils before they can be effectively used to spread darkness. Those who have fallen victims do not know they are already possessed by the spirits of darkness as they get addicted to seeing the items. They will find it very hard if not impossible to be free from the sexual ecstasy they derive from such items. Quite a good number of victims take it as freedom to do whatever they wish with themselves just as Satanists normally say, *"do as thou will."* It is not a strange phenomenon for all victims of prince of darkness to assume that breaking the law of God is actually freedom. Of course, there is no such freedom anywhere without rules. The kind of freedom Satanism and cult religions offer is actually strong chains that bound victims to Satan just as the spider web that captures its prey.

From all the cases that are studied by researchers through out the history of man, there is no real freedom outside the life in Jesus Christ. Any other thing outside Jesus Christ is actually slavery. One of the major proofs of satanic slavery lies in the fact that slaves who are described by the Bible passage below as workers of iniquities are without peace.

The Bible says in Isaiah 59:1-10, *"Behold, the LORD'S hand is not shortened, that it cannot save; neither his ear heavy, that it cannot hear: But your iniquities have separated between you and your God, and your sins have hidden his face from you, that he will not hear. For your hands are defiled with blood, and your fingers with iniquity; your lips have spoken lies, your tongue has muttered perverseness. None calls for justice, nor any pleads for truth: they trust in vanity, and speak lies; they conceive mischief, and bring forth iniquity. They hatch cockatrice' eggs, and weave the spider's web: he that eats of their eggs dies, and that which is crushed breaks out into a viper. Their webs shall not become garments, neither shall they cover themselves with their works: their works are works of iniquity, and the act of violence is in their hands. Their feet run to evil, and they make haste to shed innocent blood: their thoughts are thoughts of iniquity; wasting and destruction are in their paths. The way of peace they know not; and there is no judgment in their goings: they have made them crooked paths: whosoever goes therein shall not know peace. Therefore is judgment far from us, neither does justice overtake us: we wait for light, but behold obscurity; for brightness, but we walk in darkness. We grope for the wall like the blind, and we grope as if we had no eyes: we stumble at noonday as in the night; we are in desolate places as dead men."*

It was clear from the above Bible passage that the workers of iniquities are under the yoke of Satan or other demons that are leading them as condemned souls to the lake that burns with fire and brimstone, according to Revelation 21:8.

The only way out this inevitable destruction is to be born-again through faith in Jesus Christ, according to John 3:16.

True freedom is actually salvation in Jesus Christ while real slavery is unrighteous life through consciously or unconsciously following the leading of Satan and the rest of the devils.

CHAPTER NINE

<u>SLAVERY AND SEX TOOLS OF SATANISM</u>

Here are two illustrations that explain the true colour of slavery in both ancient and modern days. One of them is as follows:

One Easter Sunday morning, a pastor who lived in a small town in England went to the Church with an old bird cage which he placed on the pulpit, making the congregation to raise eyebrows.

In response to their puzzled expressions, the pastor began to tell the people what happened.

'I was walking through the town yesterday when I saw a young boy coming towards me, swinging this bird cage. On the bottom of the cage were three little wild birds, shivering with cold and fright.

'I stopped him and asked, "what do you have there, son?"

'"Just some old birds," came the reply.

'"What are you going to do with them?" I asked.

'"Take them home and have fun with them," he answered. "I'm going to tease them and pull out their feathers to make them fight. I'm going to have a real good time."

'"But you'll get tired of those birds sooner or later. What will you do then?"

'"Oh, I've got some cats," he said. "They like birds. I'll take them to them." '

The pastor was silent for moment. "How much do you want for those birds, son?"

'"Huh! Why? You don't want the birds, mister. They are just plain old field birds. They don't sing. They are not even pretty!"

'"How much?" The pastor asked again.

The boy sized up the pastor as if he was crazy and said, "ten pounce?"

The pastor counted and placed the amount in the boy's hand. In a flash, the boy was gone. The pastor let out the birds and brought the empty cage to the Church.

This story can be turned into the illustration of Jesus Christ and Satan like this:

Satan just returned from the Garden of Eden, and he was gloating and boasting. 'Yes, sir, I just caught a world, full of people down there. I set a trap, used a bait which I knew they couldn't resist. I got them all! Yeepeee!'

'What are you going to do with them?' Jesus asked Satan.

He replied, 'oh, I'm going to have fun. I'll teach them to marry and divorce. I'll teach them how to hate and abuse each other, drink, smoke, commit fornication and do all sorts of things. I'm going to teach them how to invent guns and bombs and kill each other. I'm really going to have fun!'

'And what will you do when you're done with them?' Jesus asked him.

'Oh, I'll kill them second time in hell fire,' Satan declared.

'How much do you want for them?' Jesus asked.

'Oh you don't want these people. They are not good. Why? You'll take them and they'll hate You. They'll spit at You, curse You and kill You. You don't want these people!'

'How much?' Jesus asked again.

Satan looked at Jesus and sneered, 'all your blood, tears and Your life!'

Jesus said, 'DONE!' Then He paid the price for the people to be free.

Everybody in this world is born into slavery and by nature and practice all human beings are slaves. In 2 Peter 2:18-19, the Bible makes us to understand that through sins, man is made a slave, making him to live in errors. While there is a promise of liberty, many still remain slaves of corruption.

The second illustration that depicts perfectly the condition of a slave is take from a movie. The story in the movie centres on a man who has lots of slaves. It seemed he did not know what to do with them. So he could afford to pick two strong men among them and tell them to start fighting each other for the purpose of the excitement and entertainment he derived from it. These two slaves who were once friends fought each other until blood started oozing out of them, making their master very excited. At a point, one of them became so weak and wounded that he could no longer fight the other man. The master told the stronger slave to strike him dead. The slave obeyed, of course, killing the other. The master congratulated the slave for being the winner in the fight against his friend.

Slaves always think they are free and save because Satan uses things they can perceive with their human senses to programme them to feel that way. He has designed the system of the world to make people see slavery as ways of normal life. Their so-called freedom inspires them to go deeper into slavery by asking for more of so-called freedom to do whatever they like, including the right to use guns to protect themselves against other slaves like them. It is when the consequences of their Satan-inspired actions dawn on them that they would realize that they are never free as they think.

The case of a drug addict who is a teenager can be used to illustrate the satanic terms for freedom.

The teenager lacks experience about life but he considers himself intelligent and smart. He felt he needed freedom from his parents and went about it by living wayward life despite warnings of its consequences. He mixed up with wrong set of people who told him to have 'open mind' so as to receive new ideas. One of the ideas was to try using drugs that would make him feel good, singing, "I believe I can fly." He tried the drug. He felt "good" about it. He tried it again and again until he got used to it without knowing he was destroying himself gradually. He became so addicted to it that he resolved into making money by all means before he could afford to buy the drugs. The feeling of freedom to do whatever he liked, which led him into drugs was what led him into crimes and other things that later claimed his life before he turned 35.

Satan works in the same way. As echoed in the secular world, he defines freedom as "doing what you want." In other words, the secular definition of freedom is an act of being free from the law of God that specifies the way to live in the world.

Having established these, there is a need to go into the all important tool of Satanism, which is sex tool.

<u>Sex Tools</u>

This can be defined as human beings that have made themselves available to be used to spread Satanism and cult religions through sex or appeal for sex, sodomy or pornographic tools. It is human beings that are used to operate in all these areas although Satan controls every tool. Human beings are used to manufacture sex appeal items like the case of Lady Gaga. They are used to make laws that

83

promote sodomy and used to pose naked in pornography such as can be seen in still and motion pictures.

Many years ago, when sex tools are not as available as they are now, demons go as far as turning into males or females with good looks and seductive bodies, sleeping around with normal human beings just like what happened in Genesis 6: 1 to 6. There are so many cases like the snake demon that can be used to establish this fact. Another case of lady demon who called herself Emily can be used.

About thirty-five years ago, a young man went to an all-night disco party where he met a very beautiful lady who called herself Emily.

He had a nice chat with her, making other young men at the party envious of him. One thing led to another until Emily took him to her "home" around 2 a.m.

She lived in a very luxurious mansion in a very splendid area. Nobody was around when they entered the house. As they entered, they were greeted with different kinds of music that uplifted his spirit.

Emily took him to her room for fun. She told him to undress which he did. As she undressed herself, there was heavy banging of the door. Another man was calling her name, "Emily! Emily!" She told the young man to pass through the window and escape. Dressed only in pants, he passed through the window and landed on a graveyard. Then it dawned on him that he had just encountered a demon from the grave that posed as a young beautiful lady. The lady demon haunted him for a very long time, according to the testimony of this man. The beautiful house in the fantastic environment was actually a graveyard. It took an anointed servant of God to deliver this young man from the lady demon.

For the purpose of this study, Sex Tools can be roughly divided into four groups, which are (i) Conscious Sex Tools (ii) Subconscious Sex Tools (iii) Unconscious Sex Tools and (iv) Invisible Sex Tools.

<u>Conscious Sex Tools</u>: The people in this category are conscious of the fact that they are sex tools when they are involved in fornication or adultery. These are people who know that having sex with others who are not their spouses is a grievous sin against God. This is especially applicable to

Christians who commit fornication or adultery. In 1 Corinthians 6:15-20, the Bible says, *"Know ye not that your bodies are the members of Christ? Shall I then take the members of Christ, and make them the members of an harlot? God forbid. What? know ye not that he which is joined to an harlot is one body? For two, saith he, shall be one flesh. But he that is joined unto the Lord is one spirit. Flee fornication. Every sin that a man does is without the body; but he that commits fornication sins against his own body. What? know ye not that your body is the temple of the Holy Ghost which is in you, which ye have of God, and ye are not your own? For ye are bought with a price: therefore glorify God in your body, and in your spirit, which are God's."*

From the above passage, conscious sex tools are people who have the following attributes:

A. They were once redeemed by Jesus Christ from Satan and delivered from destruction (Galatians 3:13).

B. Their bodies were once temple of the Holy Spirit (1 Corinthians 3:16)

C. They defile their bodies with sin of sexual immoralities (1 Corinthians 3:17)

D. Through sexual immoralities, they grieve the Holy Spirit in their lives. (1 Thessalonians 5:19)

Conscious sex tools know they are empty spiritually, if not yet completely possessed with spirit of sexual immoralities but they cannot help making themselves available for others who are not their spouses to be used as sex tools. Most of these people still believe they are still Christians even though their sexual relationships with others are directly opposed by the word of God.

Subconscious Sex Tools: In Hebrew 11:31, the Bible talks of the faith of a harlot called Rahab who although did not believe but took steps of faith. Going by this passage, subconscious sex tools can be explained as people who know that being involved in sexual immoralities is wrong but feel helpless about it. They may not necessarily be Christians but, deep inside them, they know being involved in sexual immoralities is bad enough. So many cultures condemn it. In fact there are some people in Africa who can kill if they discover that their spouses are cheating on them. There was a criminal case of a man who murdered three people, including his wife, her mother and the man that was having sex with the wife.

Actually, Satan uses most people all over the world as sex tools after he conditions their minds to accept sexual immoralities as part of the normal life. He influences people, especially virgins to place less value on their virginity. When a female is about to lose her virginity, she often times bleeds a little. The blood represents a covenant. If it is her husband that takes her virginity, the covenant is a holy one between the woman and the man with God as a witness. However, if the man it is not her husband, it becomes an unholy covenants between Satan and the two sexual partners. There is a case that establishes this as a fact, which may not be so common.

A 24-year old man manipulated a virgin of 18 to surrender her seductive body to him. After he took her away virginity, the girl cleaned the blood that ran down her thigh with one of her left fingers. She told him to lick the blood on the finger. To make her happy and thinking it was nothing, the man licked the blood with his tongue. Of course, the act resulted into an unholy covenant that bound the two of them together for life. It so bound them that when he had sex with another woman, he was struck with terrible sickness that defy treatments. It took the confession of the young lady before he realized that he must not have sex with another person if he wanted to stay alive. This forced him to marry her.

With unholy covenant through sexual intercourse, a person is made a subconscious sex tool by sometimes making herself or himself available to be used for the purpose of sexual immoralities. Some go to the extreme of not feeling comfortable if they do not have sex in a day. Some also go as far as sleeping with as many partners as possible. To make it obvious that the spirits of darkness are at work in their lives, even at the age they are supposed to be pissed off by sex, some people still flirt around like street dogs. There was man of about eighty-five who boasted that he satisfied his twenty-five year old woman with sex nearly every day. Out of curiosity, the author questioned the woman who confirmed the claim. She even wondered where he got the strength from. The elderly man was questioned how he was able to sexually satisfy the woman at that age. His explanations indicated that his source of sexual urge was demonic. This case may be a little rare but the commonest ones are sixty year old women and above still getting involved in prostitution.

The subconscious sex tools know that their involvements in sexual immoralities are injurious to their bodies or spirit being or even destructive to their souls. Still, out of sheer sexual excitements or for commercial purposes, which are always orchestrated by Satan, they journey deeper into sexual destruction.

<u>Unconscious Sex Tools:</u> People in this category are so common that they are almost in every home all over the world. They are also in every profession and every walk of life. This group of people is spiritually dead (disconnected the source of real life), going by the passage in 1 Timothy 5:6, which says, *"But she that lives in pleasure is dead while she lives."* The very thing that causes destruction is what these people delight in doing. They believe sex is a pleasurable thing which everybody in the world can always enjoy anyhow, anyway and with anyone. These people are not only dead spiritually but also serve as tools to spread and promote Sexually Transmitted Destruction to others.

The recent trend of sexual promiscuities is that adultery is allowed in some countries. This means that man or woman no longer has the right to repudiate his or her spouse because of adultery. The United States confirms that for all other countries in the world to build good relations with the great power, these countries must practice homosexual marriage. Some countries make law that prohibits incest of no value while some cities are made places of public sex. While some countries also allow bestiality (sex with animals), some allows pornographic films in high schools and universities with some authorizing prostitution of minors.

Aside from the above sex tools that receive legal backings, a good number of sex tools such as music stars openly confess to the world that they have sold their souls to Satan, thereby influencing their fans to be sexually promiscuous. Everyone of them seems to be competing with one another in the promotion of sex and obscenities through songs and movies. They are so unconscious of the fact that they are human beings, not animals. So many things may be responsible for their states of minds, which may include any of the followings:

1. Their souls are not reached with the word of God early enough before they are caught in the satanic web of lies. In 1 Timothy 2:24-26, however, the Bible says, *"And a servant of the Lord must not quarrel (with those who disagree with them) but be gentle to all, able to teach, patient, in humility correcting those who are in opposition, if God perhaps will grant them repentance, so that they may know the truth, and that they may come to their senses and escape the snare of the devil, having been taken captive by him to do his (the devil's) will."*

2. Somewhere along the line, the unconscious sex tool picks the wrong role model like the case of Rihanna, "The Good Girl Gone Bad" who said that her greatest idol is Beyonce. So it is a little wonder how a good girl went bad after picking a music star who had sold her soul to the devil. In 1 Peter 2:21, the Bible says, *"for to this you were called, because Christ also suffered for us, leaving us an example, that you should follow His steps."* In order words, anyone who takes Jesus Christ as his or her role model cannot fall victims of Satan.

3. Satan has so many servants that pose as Christian leaders whose main function is to mislead the people into Satanism and cult religions like the deposed Pope Benedict, Joseph Ratzinger. There are so many cases of people who are lost right in the church. In one of the author's books titled: Insanity Of Humanity, he researched the subject of brainwashing and came into the conclusion that brainwashed persons, especially the ones that are brainwashed with religion often do not know that they are brainwashed. In fact, they will seek to brainwash others since they are brainwashed and programmed to deceive. In 2 Timothy 3:13, the Bible says, *"but evil men and seducers shall wax worse and worse, deceiving, and being deceived."*

CHAPTER TEN

SATANISM IN GOVERNMENT - CASE STUDY OF THE ILLUMINATI CONTROL

Dr Henry Makow in his interview with Svalis reports, *"A woman who was raised in illuminati cult describes a powerful secret organization comprising one percent of the US population that has infiltrated all social institutions and covertly preparing at military takeover. Her revelations cast the 'war on terror' and 'homeland security' in their true light.*

"Svali is the pseudonym of the woman age 45 (as at the time of this report). She was a mind programmer for the cult until 1996. She was the sixth head trainer in the San Diego branch and had 30 trainers reporting to her. She has risked her life to warn humanity of the illuminati covert power and agenda.

"She describes a sadistic satanic cult led by the richest and most powerful people in the world. It is largely homosexual and pedophile, practices animal sacrifices and ritual murder. It works 'hand in glove' with CIA freemasonry. It is Aryan Supremacist (German is spoken at the top) but welcomes Jewish apostates. It controls the world traffic in drugs, guns, pornography and prostitution. It may be the hand behind political assassination, and 'terrorism', including September 11, the Maryland snippet and the Bali bomb blast.

"It has infiltrated government on a local, state and national level; education and financial institutions, religions and the media. Based in Europe, it plans a world that will make its earlier attempts, Nazism and communism look like picnics. One other detail: these people are not happy.

"Svali's courageous testimony explains why our children are no longer taught Civic Values, why they are being habituated to homosexuality and violence and why our 'culture' is descending into nihilism and sexual depravity. It raises the possibility that George W. Bush and his administration are illuminists and much of the world 'elites' are engaged in a mind-boggling criminal conspiracy.

"In March 2000, Svali began writing a monthly column for

survivors of illuminati ritual abuse at Suite 101.com. In December 2000, H.J Springer, the editor of centrExNews.com contacted Svali and conducted an interview with her by email, which is reproduced online and is copyrighted."

Dr Henry Makow is convinced of Svali's testimony just like many others like Springer who wrote, *"I have personally replied numerous email messages to her from other members... ritually abused, brainwashed, raped, sexually abused people and name it... Some of them confirming to me her story. So I have absolutely no doubt that Svali has been part of the illuminati since childhood. "*

Henry who had been making intensive research on these issues ascertains that everything fits: From the dead hand that seems to suppress humanity to why Clinton gave secret technology to The Chinese, to persistent reports of concentration camps in the U.S. It explains why people he knows behave in a conspirational way.

Addressing the question of illuminati taking over the world, Svali says that the illuminati are present in every major metropolitan centre in the United States. The Illuminati believes in controlling an area through its banks and financial institutions. They are sitting on banking board, local government, local city council, law. Children are encouraged to go to law school, medical school. Others are also encouraged to go journalism school, and members help fund local papers.

The illuminati is a group that practices form of faith known as "enlightenment". It is Luciferian, and they teach their followers to go back to the ancient mystery religions of Babylon, Egypt, and Celtic druidism. They have taken what they consider the "best" of each other, the foundational sacrifices, and joined them together into a strong occult discipline. Many groups at the local level worship ancient deities such as "El", "Baal", and "Ashtarte" as well as "Isis, Osiris" and "Set"...

According to Svali, Weishaupt did not create the illuminati, they chose him as a figurehead and told him what to write about. The financiers, dating back to the bankers during the times of the Templar Knights who financed the early kings in Europe, created the "Illuminati". Weishaupt was their "gofer", who did their bidding.

"Briefly, each region of the United States has "nerve centres" or power bases for regional activity. The United States has been divided up into seven major geographical religions. Each region has localities within it that contain military compounds and bases that are hidden in remote, isolated areas or on large private estates.

These bases are used intermittently to teach and train generational illuminati in military techniques hand-to-hand combat, crowd control, use of arms, and all aspects of military warfare. Illuminists believe that the governments of most nations around the world are destined to collapse. These will be planned collapses, and they will occur in the following ways:

The illuminati has planned first for financial collapse that will make the great depression look like picnic. This will occur through the maneuvering of the great banks and financial institutions of the world through stock manipulation and interest rate charges. Most people will be indebted to the federal government through banks and credit cards, debit etc. The government will recall all debts immediately, but most people will be unable to pay and will be bankrupted. This will cause generalized financial panic, which will occur simultaneously worldwide, as the illuminists firmly believe in controlling people through finances. The good news is that if a person is debt-free, owes nothing to the government or credit debt and can live self sufficiently, they may do better than others. One can invest in gold, not stocks if he has the income. Gold will once again be the world standard, and dollars will be pretty useless...

"Next there will be a military takeover, region by region, as the government declares a state of emergency and martial law. People would have panicked, there will be an anarchical state in most localities, and the government will justify its move as being necessary control panicked citizens. The cult trained military leaders and people under their direction will use arms as well as crowd control techniques to implement this new state of affairs... Military bases will be set up in each locality (actually, they are already here, but are covert.) In the next few years, they will go above the ground and be revealed. Each locality will have regional bases and leaders to which they are accountable. The hierarchy will closely

reflect the current convert hierarchy."

About five years after Svali left the illuminati, approximately 1% of the US population was either part of the illuminati, sympathetic to it, or a victim of mind control (and therefore considered useable.) While this number may not sound like many, imagine 1% of population highly trained in the use of armaments, crowd control, psychological and behavioral techniques, armed with weapons and linked to paramilitary groups.

"The national council consists of influential bankers with old money such as: The Rockefellers, the Mellon family, the Carnegie family, the Rothschild family etc.

"The supreme world council is already set up as a prototype of the one that will rule when the new world order comes into being. It meets on regular basis to discuss finances, direction, policy, etc and to problem-solve difficulties that come up once again, these leaders are heads in the financial world, old banking money: The Rothschild family in England, and in France, have ruling seats. A descendant of the Hapsburg dynasty has a generational seat. A descendant of the ruling families of the England and France have a generational seat. The Rockefellers family in the US holds a seat.

"This is one reason that the illuminati have been pretty untouchable over the years. The ruling members are very, very, very wealthy and powerful. Every illuminati child is taught who their 'leaders' are, and told to take an oath of allegiance to them and the 'New Order to come'."

Svali further explains that the UN was created early in the century in order to help overcome one of the biggest barriers to a one-world government... *"That barrier is the one of nationalism, or pride is one's country. This is why it was not a popular concept when first introduced. It took years of country bashing in the media and the destruction of any sense of national pride by a (not of subtle) media campaigns over the years.*

"The UN is a preparation, but it is not the real power in the world, and will be relatively unimportant when the New World Order comes into being. The real council will then step forward. But as a means of getting the general public to accept the idea of a 'global community' and the 'one world

community', the UN is a stepping stone in their working towards the New World Order.

"The conflict in the Middle East is only to the advantage of the illuminist. They HATE Israel, and hope one day to see it destroyed... One of the olive branches offered by the UN when it takes over is that they will prevent war in the Middle East, and this will be greeted with joy of many. At the same time, the illuminati covertly supply guns and funds to BOTH sides to keep the conflict fueled. They are very duplicitous people. They used to funnel guns through the USSR to Palestine, for example, in the name of promoting "friendliness" between the USSR and this state and the other Arab nations. Then, the US illuminists would help funnel guns to Israel, for the same reason. These people love the game of chess, and see warfare between nations as creating an order of chaos. The USSR is going to get stronger again. It has too strong a military both openly, and covertly. (All illuminati military trainers have visited Russia to learn from them) to sit quietly and quiescently to the side. In the New World Order, they will be stronger than US.

"In response to the question if the illuminatia Jewish conspiracy, Svali says that it is absolutely not. In fact, Hitler and his people, especially Himmler and Goebbels were top illuminists. The illuminati are racist in the extreme. As a child, Svali was forced to play "concentration camp" both on her farm in Virginia, and also in Europe in isolate camps in Germany.

"The Nazi/concentration camp mentality is very strong, though, and Svali was told that Hitler, Himmler, Goebbel, and others were high-ranking German members of the group (Himmler was higher than the other two), and Mengele their paid puppets as well, who later worked as a high trainer of the American branch between his periods of hiding in South America. They honestly believed that they were acting as agents of their 'gods' to exterminate the Jewish race. This group has enacted so many horrors on the earth."

However anyone may feel about Henry Makow's interview with Svalis, which pointed out the plan for the New World Order, a few points are confirmed by William Guy Carr in his book titled: "Pawn In The Game". The followings are excerpts from the book:

"If what I reveal surprises and shocks the reader, please don't develop an inferiority complex because I am frank to admit that although I have worked since 1911, trying to find out why the Human Race can't live in peace and enjoy the bounties and blessing God provides for our use and benefit in such abundance? It was 1950 before I penetrated the secret that the wars and revolutions which scourge our lives, and the chaotic conditions that prevail, are nothing more or less than the effects of the continuing Luciferian conspiracy. It started in that part of the universe we call heaven when Lucifer challenged The Right of God to exercise supreme authority. The Holy Scriptures tell us how the Luciferian conspiracy was transferred to this world in the Garden of Eden. Until I realized that our struggle is not with flesh and blood, but with the spiritual forces of darkness who control all those in high places on this earth (Eph. 6:12) the pieces of evidence gathered all over this world just didn't fit together and make sense. (I am not ashamed to admit that the "Bible" provided the "Key" which enabled me to obtain an answer to the question quoted above.)

"...The Luciferian ideology states might is right. It claims being of proven superior intelligence have the right to rule those less gifted because the masses don't know what is best for them. The Luciferian ideology is what we call totalitarianism to-day.

"The Old Testament is simply the history of how Satan became prince of the world, and caused our first parents to defect from God. It relates how the synagogue of Satan was established on this earth, it tells how it has worked since to prevent God's Plan for the rule of the universe being established on this earth. Christ came to earth when the conspiracy reached the stage that, to use his own words, Satan controlled all those in high places. He exposed the synagogue of Satan (Revelation 2:9; 3:9;) He denounced those who belonged to it as sons of the devil (Lucifer), whom He castigated as the father of lies (John 8:44) and the prince of deceit (2 Corinthians 11:14). He was specific in His statement that those who comprised the synagogue of Satan were those who called themselves Jews, but were not, and did lie (Revelation 2:9; 3:9). He identified the Money-Changers (Bankers) the Scribes, and the Pharisees as the

Illuminati of His day. What so many people seem to forget, is the fact that Christ came on earth to release us from the bonds of Satan with which we were being bound tighter and tighter as the years rolled by. Christ gave us the solution to our problem when he told us we must go forth and teach the truth, regarding this conspiracy (John 8. 31:59;), to all people of all nations. He promised that if we did this, knowledge of the truth would set us free (Matthew 28:19;). The Luciferian Conspiracy has developed until it is in its semi-final stage (Matthew 24: 15:34;), simply because we have failed to put the mandate Christ gave us into effect.

"In 1784 "An Act of God" placed the Bavarian government in possession of evidence which proved the existence of the continuing Luciferian Conspiracy. Adam Weishaupt, a Jesuit-trained

"Professor of Canon Law, defected from Christianity, and embraced the Luciferian ideology while teaching in Ingoldstadt University. In 1770 the money lenders (who had recently organized the House of Rothschild), retained him to revise and modernize the age-old 'protocols' designed to give the Synagogue of Satan ultimate world domination so they can impose the Luciferian ideology upon what remains of the Human Race, after the final social cataclysm, by use of satanic despotism. Weishaupt completed his task May 1st, 1776.

"The plan required the destruction of ALL existing governments and religions. This objective was to be reached by dividing the masses, whom he termed Goyim (meaning human cattle) into opposing camps in ever increasing numbers on political, racial, social, economic and other issues. The opposing sides were then to be armed and an 'incident' provided which would cause them to fight and weaken themselves as they destroyed National Governments and Religious Institutions.

"In 1776 Weishaupt organized the Illuminati to put the plot into execution.

"The word "Illuminati" is derived from Lucifer, and means 'holders of the light'. Using the lie that his objective was to bring about a One World Government to enable men with proven mental ability to govern the world, he recruited about two thousand followers. These included the most intelligent

men in the field of Arts and Letters: Education: the sciences, finance and industry. He then established Lodges of the Grand Orient to be their secret headquarters. Weishaupt's revised plan required his Illuminati to do the following things to help them accomplish their purpose.

(1) Use monetary and sex bribery to obtain control of people already occupying positions in high places in the various levels of ALL governments and other fields of human endeavour. Once an influential person had fallen for the lies, deceits, and temptations of the Illuminati they were to be held in bondage by application of political and other forms of blackmail and threats of financial ruin, public exposure, and physical harm and even death to themselves and their loved ones.

(2) Illuminati on the faculties of colleges and universities were to recommend students possessing exceptional mental ability belonging to well bred families with international leanings for special training in internationalism. This training was to be provided by granting scholarships to those selected. They were to be educated (indoctrinated) into accepting the 'Idea' that only a One World Government can put an end to recurring wars and tribulations. They were to be at first persuaded and then convinced that men of special abilities and brains had the RIGHT to rule those less gifted, because the Goyim (masses of the people) don't know what is best for them physically, mentally and spiritually. Today three such special schools are located in Gordonstoun in Scotland; Salem in Germany; and Anavryta in Greece. Prince Phillip, the husband of Queen Elizabeth of England, was educated at Gordonstoun at the instigation of Lord Louis Mountbatten, his Uncle, who became Britain's Admiral of the Fleet after World War Two ended.

(3) Influential people trapped into coming under the control of the Illuminati, and students who had been specially educated and trained were to be used as agentur and placed behind the scenes of ALL governments as "Experts" and "Specialists" so they could advise the top executives to adopt policies which would in the long run, serve the secret plans of the One Worlders and bring about the ultimate destruction of the governments and religions they were elected or appointed to serve.

(4) The Illuminati were to obtain control of the Press and all other agencies which distribute information to the public. News and information was to be slanted so that the Goyim would come to believe that a One World Government is the ONLY solution to our many and varied problems. Because Britain and France were the two greatest powers at the end of the 18th Century, Weishaupt ordered the Illuminati to foment the Colonial Wars to weaken the British Empire and organize the Great Revolution to weaken the French Empire. The latter he scheduled should start in 1789.

"A German author named Zwack put Weishaupt's revised version of the age-old conspiracy into book form and named it "Einige Original-Scripten." In 1784 a copy of this document was sent to the Illuminists Weishaupt had delegated to foment the French revolution. The courier was struck dead by lightning as he rode through Ratisbon on his way from Frankfurt to Paris. The police found the subversive documents on his body and turned them over to the proper government authorities.

After careful study of the plot, the Bavarian Government ordered the police to raid Weishaupt's newly organized lodges of the Grand Orient and the homes of some of his most influential associates, including the castle of Baron Bassus-in-Sandersdorf. Additional evidence thus obtained convinced the authorities the documents were a genuine copy of a conspiracy by which the synagogue of Satan, who controlled the Illuminati AT THE TOP, planned to use wars and revolutions to bring about the establishment of one kind or another of a One World Government, the powers of which they intended to usurp as soon as it was established.

In 1785, the Bavarian Government outlawed the Illuminati and closed the lodges of the Grand Orient. In 1786, they published the details of the conspiracy. The English title is "The Original Writtings of the Order and Sect of The Illuminati". Copies of the conspiracy were sent to the heads of church and state. The power of the Illuminati was so great that this warning was ignored, as were the warnings Christ had given the world.

The Illuminati went underground. Weishaupt instructed his Illuminists to infiltrate into the lodges of Blue Masonry and form a secret society within secret societies. Only masons who proved themselves Internationalists, and those whose conduct proved they had defected from God, are initiated into the Illuminati. Thus the conspirators used the cloak of philanthropy to hide their revolutionary and subversive activities. In order to infiltrate into Masonic Lodges in Britain, Illuminists invited John Robison over to Europe. He was a high degree mason in the Scottish Rite: Professor of natural philosophy at Edinburgh University; and Secretary of The Royal Society of Edinburgh. John Robison did not fall for the lie that the objective of the one worlders was to form a benevolent dictatorship. He kept his reactions to himself however, and was entrusted with a copy of Weishaupt's Revised Conspiracy for study and safe keeping. Because the heads of church and state in France were advised to ignore the warnings given them, the revolution broke out in 1789. In order to alert other governments to their danger, in 1798 John Robison published a book, entitled "Proof of a Conspiracy to Destroy All Governments and Religions". But his warnings have been ignored, as were the others."

What is instructive to note in the results of all these research works through reports, including news items, interviews, including Henry Makow's with Svalis and William Guy Carr's assertions is that Satanism and cult regions are real. Part of the proofs that Satanism is in all governments can be observed through attitudes and speeches of world leaders, especially towards terrorism.

Using the United States as a case study, the news reports indicated that terrorism is Satanism in government. The compelling proofs attribute terrorism to the involvements of governments. With so much government secrets, cover-ups and compromise of the constitution, finding out the truth about Satanism in governments does not require thorough researched works. Taking the case of 911 terrorism to justify the 'war on terror' for instance, it was argued by people who are considered conspiracy theorists that the collapses of the Towers, which served as world trade centre were attributed to controlled demolition. When the official report stated that the Towers fell due to severe structural damage caused by the hijacked planes and resulting into fire, it was argued that the fire did not burn long enough (56 minutes in the case of the

South Towers) to cause the catastrophic collapse. Moreover, the way the buildings fell so quickly and perfectly with reports of explosives being heard before the Towers collapsed and debris visibly shooting out from the lower levels of buildings suggested an inside job. Secondly, besides the Twin Towers, one more building in the Trade Centre complex collapsed without being hit by any plane. It only caught fire and burnt for some hours with no fire fighters coming to rescue the building until it fell at free speed for the first few seconds of its collapse. Prior to 911, no steel-framed high rise building had ever collapse because of fire. From circumstantial evidences, therefore, if planes or fire did not cause the collapse, then the only logical explanation is a controlled demolition which implicates high-level US Government officials.

It is also observed that the real cause of civil wars and much bloodshed in so many countries all over the world cannot be ascertained or justified. There are so many rebels in some countries like Syria, Iran, Iraq and many others; including the ones in Africa who are being funded from the outside to fight their governments. Nearly in all conflict zones continue to be ravaged with wars until the United Nation establishes its presence in the countries. Once it is there, the UN never leaves the country even after conflicts had been resolved.

Through financial institutions that enslave countries through national debts, assassinations of presidents that never support them in their quest to dominate the world and through creation of terrorism, Satanists in whatever names they are called - be it illuminati, Freemasons, Bones and Skulls, they are able to have governments in nearly all over the world in their pockets. Groups of Satanists are working tirelessly to bring all governments together under one control, going by testimonies of defectors. They have been trying to do this right from one generation to another but they keep failing all the time. The mere fact that Satanists never give up trying to execute their age-long plans does not mean they will keep failing. Going through the predictions of the Bible, they will succeed only at an appointed time of God.

The next chapter will perhaps shed light on what God says about the condition in the world.

CHAPTER ELEVEN

THE CONDITION OF THE WORLD ACCORDING TO THE WORD OF GOD - THE BIBLE

To first establish what is really the word of God among so many books that claim to be God's word or holy books, there is need to consider the classical case study of Darren Hewer who shared his testimony that goes as follows:

"I grew up without any religious education, and only knew as much Christianity as I was able to pick up from culture and the media - not much! When I was younger, I had some sort of vague belief in God, but I knew nothing of Christianity or any other faiths. As I got older, I started to adopt an atheistic attitude, mostly because my friends at the time were atheists, not due to any particular reason or life circumstances.

"As I neared the completion of my degree in Information System & Human Behaviour, I started to feel that something was missing in my life. By all accounts I had things pretty good. I generally didn't have to worry about money, I was doing well in school, and had a loving family. Yet, I felt depressed. I decided to make a list of things I wanted to try in order to find out what that 'missing part' of my life was. One of the items on the list was to investigate religion (and God) for the first time. I figured it was worth a shot and wouldn't cost me anything. It'd be at least a good learning opportunity. So I decided to investigate various religions to see whether any of them were credible. I can't recall all of the faith that I looked at, but I definitely spent more time with Buddhism, Hinduism, Islam, Mormonism and Christianity. I wanted a faith that was true: Something that made me feel good but was not grounded in reality was not worth considering.

"As far as I can recall, the first religion I looked ay was Buddhism. I had a positive impression dif Buddhism, probably from the positive way it is usually portrayed in the media. I never heard Buddhism being criticized. It seems to be the most 'socially acceptable' religion. (Social acceptance is hardly the best test for truth! But such was my thinking at the time.)

"Buddhism is atheistic; at least, the question of God's

existence is said to be peripheral to Buddhist faith. Some Buddhists believe God exists, but many don't. To me, any religion that is atheistic is not a religion at all, it is merely a philosophy, invented by humankind and therefore no better or worse than any other philosophy (at least in terms of potential for error). If a religion differs within itself so widely on the most central topic of faith (whether or not God exists) it's difficult to even call it one faith at all. How could Buddha have been so misunderstood that his followers could not agree on the most basic question of whether God exists or not, and whether that maters? (I would say yes God does exists, and yes it does matter... But we haven't quite come to the point yet!)

"I read about the various leaders of religions; for example, Muhammad of Islam, Joseph Smith of Mormonism and Jesus of Christianity.

"I was somewhat surprised by what I discovered. All claimed to have the right answer, the 'only way', but Jesus was the only one who claimed to BE GOD!

"Why follow mere men, who would be filled with error, instead of God himself, in whom there would be no error? The gospel story really spoke to me in a way that the stories of Islam and Mormonism (and others) didn't. If any of these stories were true, I wanted Christianity to be true but, the question was whether it really was true or not. So I figured I'd spend more time investigating it. The person of Jesus Christ struck me as being authentic, in a way that the others didn't. And I knew that it was quite impossible for ALL of these faiths to be true. (Clearly I'm not a 'postmodernist'). If I accepted Jesus, I couldn't accept the rest.

"I needed to carefully investigate the Christian faith before accepting it. I had some Christian friends at the time, but I didn't tell any of them that I was reading about Christianity because if I decided that Christianity wasn't true, I didn't want to tell them that their religion is a fairytale.

"I was still wary of the Church, so I bought myself a copy of the Bible and started reading it for myself. Not knowing much about the Bible and started reading at the beginning like any other book I'd read. I wondered when Jesus came into the story, and after slipping around a bit I figured out the difference between the Old and the New Testaments.

"Roughly speaking, the Old Testament is before Jesus, the New Testament is about Jesus and the early Church.

"I continued reading over the next few weeks, and although pretty skeptical about the miracle stories, I was still interested enough to continue. (I also know that if God exists, miracles are at least possible, though I had never had much confidence in them being actual before). Over the course of three months I read most of the New Testament and a large portion of the Old Testament.

"During that time I started to question the historical reliability of the Bible. If this book were true (that is, historically accurate) it certainly would be the 'greatest story ever told'. But if it weren't, it'd be no better than J.R.R Tolkien or Douglas Adams: Fine fiction, but in no sense 'holy' nor 'history'.

"I finally admitted to a close Christian friend that I had been reading the Bible, and had questions about its reliability. She gave me a book called 'The Case For Christ' by a Yale Law School graduate and former Chicago Times legal editor Lee Strobel, which examines hard questions about the reliability of the Bible. I learned to my surprise that yes, there are good reasons for believing that the Bible is reliable in what it records! My later reading has only confirmed this.

"The New Testament is the most scrutinized literature in the history of the world, and its reliability is unparalleled compared to all other documents from its time!

"Now I really began to struggle! In a way I wanted this amazing message so be true. But in another way, I really didn't. As unhappy as I was with my life, becoming a follower of Jesus would mean I'd have to make some changes and give up some of the sins that, frankly, I enjoyed. After about four months of daily reading and study (of the Bible) I had come to realize something like an intellectual acceptance, but not an acceptance in my heart. It's one thing to make a mental assent and say 'yes', I believe that this is likely to be true but it's quite another to make the more real life altering decision to change my life course and admit that for the first 20 years of my life that I had been wrong!

"In early January of 2003 I decided that I'd attend an on campus 'Church' service. I figured this would be like going to Church but not quite as weird, and I should be at least see

what Church is like. The service wasn't weird as I thought it would be, although there was a lot of singing which I didn't enjoy at the time. (I wasn't quite sure that I agreed with what they were singing about!) But when the speaker gave his short message something that he said resonated with me. He talked about having a "wow moment" with God, an experience where God speaks to you personally. I realized that was what was stopping me from accepting Christ.

"I had already rationally accepted Christian belief, but even then I knew that there was more to faith than simple intellectual ascent. I had never had a personal experience of God. So that same night, I prayed for God to personally come to me in some way. I didn't know what, if anything, to expect.

"The next night I was up later and picked up my Bible to read a bit. My Bible included some extra commentary and stories, and the story that I read involved a lonely farmer.

"One raw winter night, a farmer heard an irregular thumping sound against his kitchen storm door. He went to a window and watch as tiny, shivering sparrows, attracted to the evident warmth inside, beat in vain against the glass. Touched, the farmer bundled up and trudged through fresh snow to open the barn door for the struggling birds. He turned on the lights and tossed some hay in the corner. But the sparrows, which had scattered in all directions when he emerged from the house, hid in the darkness, afraid.

"The man tried various tactics to get them into the barn. He laid down a trail of saltine cracker crumbs to direct them. He tried circling behind the birds to drive them to the barn. Nothing worked. He, a huge, alien creature had terrified them; the birds couldn't comprehend that he actually desired to help. The farmer withdrew to his house and watched the doomed sparrows through a window. As he stared, a thought hit him like lightening from a clear blue sky: If only I could become a bird - one of them - just for a moment. Then I wouldn't frighten them so. I could show them the way to warmth and safety.

"At the same moment, another thought dawned on him. He gasped the reason Jesus was born. (As told by Paul Harvey).

"When I read this story this time, it was different than when I read it before. I felt emotion welling up inside of me, and by the time I'd read the last sentence, I was crying. Hot tears of

pain, but tears of profound joy. I'm not someone who cries easily! But here I was, alone in my room at 3 am, crying! I didn't know what was going on until I remembered my prayer from the previous night ... I finally... made a decision that would change my life. I said 'yes' to God."

There is need to note the followings, going by this case study about Christianity and others:

Firstly, Christianity is not a religion. So it must not be considered one of the religions in the world. As earlier pointed out, there are millions of lives whose lives had been transformed by the word of God while at the same time so many had unsuccessfully attacked the Bible over the years. The lives of so many people who are transformed by the word of God and the series of failed attacks on Bible up to the present days continue to prove to the world that Christianity is not a religion but a way of life as designed by God. The lives that are transformed by Jesus Christ from spiritual death into life and from the path of hell to heaven establish what Jesus said in John 14:6. He said, *"I am the Way, the Truth, and the Life. No one comes to the Father except through Me."* If Jesus is the way, it means Christianity is a way of life as established by God, the Father.

The second thing to note, especially in the above case study is the claim of founders of all religions. Nearly all, if not all founders of religions claimed to be the right way or the prophets or messengers of God but none of them claims to be God. The ones among the few that dared to claim to be God are immediately proved wrong either before or after their deaths.

The founders of most religions have links with devils either in the category of principalities, powers, rulers of darkness or spiritual hosts of wickedness. All religions with exception of none are designed by Satan with the objectives of improvising for the presence of Almighty God in the life of man. Hence they are satanic even though some of them may appear to be holy or true. The Bible pointed this out in 2 Corinthian chapter 11 verse 14, *"And no wonder! For Satan himself transforms himself into an angel of light."*

After the studies of biographies of many founders of religions, it is discovered that all of them were deceived when they encountered demons that transformed themselves into angels of light. The deceived founders of religions begin to deceive their followers, making them to worship Satan and making them think they worship God. Because these demons are powerful and tactical in the way they deceive and deal with man, most people continue to move away from God, thinking they are moving close to Him. They become Satanists through cult religions without ever suspecting it. Somehow, a lot of people practicing cult religions sometimes discover that they have been deceived when they get to certain levels in cultism but they always feel it is too late to back out. They would have been brainwashed to think they can never opt out of Satanism or cult religions at certain level.

Going by the results of this research work, Satanism and all cult religions are governed with deceptions that are used as weapons to cajole people into the practice. They also use the weapons of lies to keep dabblers or victims to climb the ladder of hierarchy and use fear to get firm grip over every member. Even when a person opts out at any level, the leaders or the rests of members of the cult declare him or her wanted - dead or alive. They always wanted them dead so that their secrets are not let out. Hundreds of thousands and even millions of defectors have received freedom and deliverance from Satanism and cult religions after they become Christians. Of course, powers which Satanism and cult religions can never contend with are given to Christians the moment they invite Jesus Christ into their lives. The basis all powers have to bow before genuine Christians is found in Philippians 2:9-11 which says, *"Therefore God also has highly exalted him and given Him the name which is above every name, that at the name of Jesus every knee should bow, of those in heaven, and of those under the earth, and every tongue should confess that Jesus Christ is Lord, to the glory of God the father."*

Findings and interviews with former top Satanists confirmed that Satan fears the name Jesus. If the name of Jesus is mentioned in the presence of Satan and other devils or demons, there are always problems among them.

During the interviews of the author with former top witches in Africa while gathering information about witchcraft for his non-fiction novel titled, "The Vessel Of Destruction", an elderly woman who is now a Christian revealed how she was flying like a bird to the meeting of witches and wizards in the middle of the night and how she got arrested on the way by a group of Christians who were praying at that time. According to her testimony, she was shot down by their prayers and then led by invisible force to their doorsteps. She was not in her physical body, which was in her house but the people could see her in the replica of her real image. She was forced to tell the Christians what happened. They led her to her house. She disappeared when they got to the door of her house and then later opened the door from inside with her physical body. This may be hard to understand but top Satanists and some of those who practice cult religions understand this kind of practice, including what is known as abstract projections with the use of demonic powers.

There are so many other cases that establish the fact that the name of Jesus causes terror to the kingdom of darkness.

Satanism is in everything that relates to the mankind, including professions, religions, politics, governments, social life, economics, entertainments, education, cultures, laws and even in some so-called Christian Churches.

Apart from studied cases, one of the things that confirm practice of Satanism and cult religion in so many Churches is found in 2 Corinthians chapter 11 verse 13 in the Bible which says, *"for such are false apostles, deceitful workers, transforming themselves into apostles of Christ."* In other words, there are some people who claim to be Christians but they are actually false. It is clear from here that Christianity has a standard, established by the word of God. Any practice that seems like Christianity but not meeting up to this standard or not conforming to the word of God is a mere religion. If any mere religion brings about manifestations of spiritual things in the physical realm such as a blind man who is made to see, it is clear demonic activities. Note that such demonic activities always involve subtle or ritual sacrifices. The kind of ritualism it involves depends on the form of cult religion.

The fact that some cult religions appear like Christianity cannot be overemphasized although this may sound controversial. This is the reason the popular case of Joseph Ratzinger, the former Catholic Pope is used as a case study.

Through this case, the height of Satanism that poses as Christianity is made clear. If Satanism can go that far, all other subtle forms of Satanism should not be a surprise. Without mentioning names of Church or denominations that are satanic, there is need study a few things about common characteristics of Satanism and cult religions, including the ones that pose as Christianity in the next chapter. Before then, it is instructive o note what the word of God says about the conditions of the world in the book of Revelation chapter 12 verse 12. It says, *"Therefore rejoice, O heavens, and you who dwell in them! Woe to the inhabitants of the earth and sea! For the devil has come down to you, having great wrath, because he knows that he has a short time."*

From the above passage, it is clear that the world is under serious satanic attack. The scourging flame of attack is emitted from the pit of hell, which is the final destination of the devils, including Satan and everyone that follows his leading.

The attack in the world is in the form of satanic stench of persecution against the people (including the Christians), Sufferings, hardships, pains, sorrow, murders, brutalities, sexual perversions and abuses, day time horrors and nightmares. Surprisingly strange enough, most people are comfortable in the midst of deaths, corruptions and rottenness. Because the environment had become impossibly hostile, a lot of Christians compromised. Some of them justify the compromise by saying, "if you can't beat them, you can join them." They do not understand that by joining them, they join forces with enemies of their souls, making themselves enemies of God. By joining them, they also join those who have made up their minds to end up in the pit of hell.

The book of Revelation 12:12 tells those who are already in heaven to rejoice because Satan who caused the war in heaven, according to Revelation 12:7-9 had been thrown out into the world. The same book of Revelation 21: 4 also gives hope to those who have decided to do everything they can to possess heaven. The passage says, *"And God shall wipe away all tears from their eyes; and there shall be no more death, neither sorrow, nor crying, neither shall there be any more pain: for the former things (the terrible things of the world, including the wars) are passed away."*

Jesus knows that Satan and other devils will make it very hard, if not impossible for people to make it to heaven, the place of eternal bliss. Hence He tells the disciples in Matthew chapter 11 verse 12, *"And from the days of John the Baptist until now the kingdom of heaven suffers violent, and the violent take it by force."*

Since what Jesus says is the reality of eternal life, it is save to conclude that this world is under serious attack. To survive it, a person must be spiritual strong and violent in prayers even after given his or her life to Jesus Christ. The people that are mostly feeling the attack are true Christians but they have been given the grace, the power and ability to become conquerors. While establishing this fact about Christians, the Bible says in Romans 8:35-39, *"Who shall separate us from the love of Christ? Shall tribulation, or distress, or persecution, or famine, or nakedness, or peril, or sword? As it is written, For your sake we are killed all the day long; we are accounted as sheep for the slaughter. No, in all these things we are more than conquerors through him that loved us. For I am persuaded, that neither death, nor life, nor angels, nor principalities, nor powers, nor things present, nor things to come, nor height, nor depth, nor any other creature, shall be able to separate us from the love of God, which is in Christ Jesus our Lord."*

CHAPTER TWELVE

<u>COMMON CHARACTERISTICS OF SATANISM AND CULT RELIGIONS</u>

The results of research works of various researchers prove that most Satanists, especially those who have mingled Satanism with Christianity do not know they are Satanists. A lot of them practice Satanism like Christianity. These groups of people may not be involved in blood sacrifices but they are involved in one ritual or the other. They may also not necessarily get involved in sex worship of Satan (like paedophilia; incest; bestiality; homosexuality etc), abuses of their victims, animal, baby and other human sacrifices, including brutalization and dismemberments of human bodies. However rigour or subtle the ritual may be, it is Satanism.

There are billions of Satanists all over the world who know they worship Satan against the commandment of God who says in Deuteronomy 5: 7-10, *"You shall have none other gods before me. You shall not make thee any graven image, or any likeness of any thing that is in heaven above, or that is in the earth beneath, or that is in the waters beneath the earth: You shalt not bow down yourself unto them, nor serve them: for I the LORD thy God am a jealous God, visiting the iniquity of the fathers upon the children unto the third and fourth generation of them that hate me, And showing mercy unto thousands of them that love me and keep my commandments."*

Satan knows much more about God than any humans both living or dead. He also knows the word of God so much that he could use it as a way to attack any man that is ignorant of it. In other to use people against God and make them to violate God's commandments, devils or demons pose as gods and goodness for them to worship.

According to ancient history, humans have ascribed various powers to supernatural beings. Such creatures include the immortal gods and goddesses. Some are given credits for the creation of the world and even mankind, or food, warfare, love, and all the other good and bad elements of life. The gods and goddess may be worshiped with alters, elaborate or gigantic statues, or sacrifices. Poets and other writers may tell stories featuring the traditional myths about the deities' involvements in human life. These vary from one society to the next. The most familiar will probably be the ones from Greek mythology which include Olympian gods.

According to Ancient Greece of the British Museum, the story of Zeus and Kronos goes as follows:

"Kronos was the king of the Titans. He was very afraid that one of his children would kill him just as he had murdered his own father. He was so worried he started to eat his own children after they were born, much to his wife's Rhea's horror!

"After the birth of their sixth child, Zeus, Rhea played a trick on Kronos. She gave him a stone to swallow instead of the baby. She hid Zeus in a cave and the young god was brought up by a goat (can one really imagine a young god being brought by a goat - a creature?)

"When Zeus was older he asked to become Kronos' cup-bearer. He put a special potion in his father's wine that caused Kronos to vomit up his children. He also vomited up the stone which he was tricked into swallowing. Then Zeus led his brothers and sisters into battle against Kronos and the Titans. Zeus became the king of the gods".

How this fantastic myth found its way into history is not really strange but a question of motive. The story just like other myths had been embedded in secular education and entertainments, including cartoons for children. As fallacious as these stories are, they have formed part of the beliefs, culminating into cult religions and worship of different gods and goddesses. From myth, often times religions are developed, proceeded by setting up of images of gods and making of sacrifices.

The story of Kronos and Zeus is the Satanic version of God, the Father, God the Son (Jesus Christ) and God the Holy Spirit. Satanists believe Satan is Zeus and God is Kronos. Unlike the case of the real God Who has no beginning and no end, the myth indicates that God murdered his own father and attempted to murder his children so that he would not be murdered. When he (Zeus) survived the murder attempt of his father (Kronos), he was able to rescue his brothers and sisters who may include Jesus Christ and Angel Michael. The studies of various brainwashing books, music and movies indicate that Satanists have very sophisticated means of perverting the truth. As pointed earlier on, with proper use of lies and deceptions, humanity is enslaved and made to serve Satan and the devils that pose as gods and goddesses, making most people ignorant of what they are doing or where they are heading after death.

However, Jesus said something very crucial to mankind in John 8:32, *"And you shall know the truth, and the truth shall make you free."* The passage indicates that mankind is enslaved with lies and deceptions for a very long. With the truth that Satan is the thief that steals, kills and destroys souls in hell, according to John 10:10, and with the truth that Jesus is the only Begotten Son of God who came to liberate mankind, according to John 3:16, anybody can be made free from Satan and other devils.

In the same gospel of John 14:6, Jesus reveals Himself as The Way out of slavery and destruction of souls, The Truth in the Bible and The Life in eternity. Everyone who is able to grasp this basic truth about Jesus Christ, however deep he or she had gone into Satanism or cult religions, he or she would be free and save from inevitable destruction that awaits those who are ignorant or who rejects the truth. But most people fail to grasp the truth because they have been deceived and fed with lies for a long time. Hence, they head towards eternal doom in hell just like shivering sparrows that failed to accept the offer of the farmer to save them from snow.

The satanic web of lies and deception is far beyond human comprehension. For one, man is limited by what he can perceive with the human senses. For two, man is ignorant of what is actually happening in the spirit realm. He only knows there is a supernatural forces but he cannot distinguish that of God and Satan. In fact, Satan uses the method of God of accepting sacrifices in the Old Testament of the Bible to further deceive the people, making them feel that they are relating with God when they are actually relating with the devils. Because Satan knows that God has moved from Old Testament to New Testament through the sacrifice of Jesus Christ, he builds another web of lies and deceptions around

Old Testament and makes some Christians get involved in worship of demons through practice of Christianity that never conform with New Testament practice. He sometimes does these by asking them to offer certain items for sacrifices such as burning of incenses or candles. As minor as these sacrifices may seem, it is a subtle way of inviting the presence of devils or invitations into enter into unholy covenant with them. Also in the process of this invitation of presence of devils through this manner, Satanism is introduced into Christianity a very subtle way. This invariably begins the practice of Satanism out of ignorance.

Though Satan is not omnipresent and omnipotent and omniscient like God, he has billions of unholy spirits working for him and tampering with the affairs of mankind. Because demons are very much around people to play the roles of God, those who mingle Satanism with Christianity begin to think they are actually serving the Almighty God. The case study of Catholicism which often times includes bowing down to the image of Virgin Mary "mother of Jesus" establishes this fact. By making images of Mary and Jesus and bowing down to them, Satanism is introduced. The higher people go in Catholicism, the deeper they are in Satanism like the deposed Pope Benedict Joseph Ratzinger. There are so many other cases of Satanism in Christianity in so many denominations and Churches which cannot be possibly listed as it grows in numbers everyday. The followings, however, can be noted as the common characteristics of Satanism and cult religions in the world.

The first noticeable characteristic is the attitudes of those who practice Satanism or cult religions towards the gospel. Although some of them claim to be Christians but when they are faced with hard truths in the Bible that reveal their inner self or identity, they become argumentative. Hence, at the subtle level, Satanists despise or pervert the Bible to suit their purposes. At the extreme level, they replace the Bible with another book like satanic Bible or other anti-Gospel literature or philosophy.

When a Christian foundation interviewed College non-believers about how and why they left religion, surprising themes emerged, according to the report of Larry Alex Taunton. The reports read as follows:

" 'Church became all about ceremony, handholding, and kumbaya,' Phil said with a look of disgust. 'I missed my old youth Pastor. He actually knew the Bible.'

"Over the course of my career I have met many students like Phil. It has been my privilege to address college students all over the world usually as one defending the Christian worldview. These events typically attract large numbers of atheists. I like that... At some point, I like to ask them a sincere question what led them to become atheists.

"Given that the New Atheism fashions itself as a movement that is ruthless by scientific, it should come as no surprise that those answering my question attribute their decisions to the purely rational objective: one involves his understanding of sciences; another says it was her exploration of the claims of this or that religious beliefs that are illogical and so on. To hear them tell it, the choices was made from a philosophically neutral position that was void of emotion...

"Atheists particularly fascinate me. Perhaps it's because I consider their philosophy - if the absence of belief may be called a philosophy - historically naive and potentially dangerous. Or maybe it's because, like any good Christian, take the big question seriously. But it was how they processed those questions that intrigued me.

"To gain some insight, we launched a nationwide campaign to interview with College students who are members of Secular Students Alliance (SSA) or Free- thought Societies (FS). These College groups are the atheist equivalents to Campus Crusade. They meet regularly for fellowship, encourage one another in their (un) belief, and even proselytize. They are people who are merely irreligious; they are actively determinedly irreligious.

"Using the fixed point formation website, email, my Twitter, and my Facebook page, we contacted the leaders of these groups and asked if they and their fellow members would participate in our study. To our surprise, we received a flood of enquires. Students ranging from Standfort University to University of Alabama-Birmingham, from Northwestern to Portland State volunteered to talk to us. The rules were simple: Tell us your journey to unbelief. It was not our purpose to dispute their stories or to debate the merits of

our views. Not then, anyway. We just wanted to listen to what they had to say. And what they had to say startled us. This brings me back to Phil.

"A smart, likable young man, he sat down nervously as my staff put a plate of food before him. Like others after him, he suspected a trap. Was he being punk'd? Talking to us required courage of all of these students, Phil most of all since he was the first to do so. Once he realized, however, that we truly meant him no harm, he started talking - and for three hours we listened.

"Now the president of his Campus's SSA, Phil was once the president of the Methodist Church's Youth group. He loved his Church (they weren't just going through the motions), his Pastor (a rock star trapped in Pastor's body) and most of all, his youth leader, Jim ('a passionate man'). Jim's Bible Studies were particularly meaningful to him. He admired the fact that Jim didn't dodge the tough chapters or the tough questions: 'He didn't always have satisfying answers or answers at all, but he didn't run away from the questions either. The way he taught the Bible made me feel smart.'

"Listening to his story I had to remind myself that Phil was an atheist, not a seminary student recalling those who had inspired him enter the pastorate. As the narrative developed, however, it became clear where things came apart from Phil. During his junior year of high school, the Church, in an effort to attract more young people, wanted Jim to teach less and pray more. Difference of opinion over this new strategy led to Jim's dismissal. He was replaced by Savannah, an attractive twenty-something who, according to Phil, 'didn't know a thing about the Bible.' The Church got what it wanted: the youth group grew. But it lost Phil.

"An hour deeper into conversation I asked, 'when did you begin to think of yourself as an atheist?'

"He thought for a moment. 'I would say by the end of my junior year.'

"I checked my notes. 'Wasn't that about the time that your Church fired Jim?'

"He seemed surprised by the connection. 'Yeah, I guess it was.'

"Phil's story, while unique in its parts, was on the whole

114

typical of the stories we would hear from students across the country. Slowly, a composite sketch of American College-aged atheists began to emerge and it would challenge all that we thought we knew about this demographic. Here is what we learned:

"They had attended Church: Most of our participants had not chosen their worldview from ideologically neutral positions at all, but in reaction to Christianity. Not Islam, not Buddhism. Christianity.

"The missions and massages of their Churches were vague: These students heard plenty of messages encouraging 'social justice, community involvement, and 'being good', but they seldom saw the relationship between the massage, Jesus Christ, and the Bible. Listen to Stephanie, a student at Northwestern:

" 'The connection between Jesus and person's life was not clear.' This is an incisive critique. She seems to intuitively understand that the Church does not exists simply to address social ills, but to proclaim the teachings of its founder, Jesus Christ, and their relevance to the world. Since Stephanie did not see that connection, she saw little incentive to stay.

"They felt their Churches offered superficial answers to life's difficult questions: When our participants were asked what they found unconvincing about the Christian faith, they spoke of evolution versus creation, sexuality, the reliability of the Biblical text, Jesus as the only way etc. Some have gone to the Church hoping to find answers to these questions of personal significance, purpose and ethics. Serious-minded, they often concluded that Church services were largely shallow, harmless, and ultimately irrelevant. As Ben, an engineering major at the University of Texas, so bluntly put it: 'I really started to get bored with the Church.'

"They expressed their respect for those ministers who took the Bible seriously: following our 2010 debate in Billings, Montana, I asked Christopher Hitchens why he didn't try to savage me on stage the way he had so many others. His reply was immediate and emphatic: 'Because you believe it.' Without fail, our former church-attending students expressed similar feelings for those Christians who unashamedly embraced Biblical teaching. Michael, a

political science major at Dartmoth, told us that he is drawn to Christians like that, adding, 'I really can't consider a Christian a good, moral person if he isn't trying to convert me.' As surprising as it may seem, this sentiment is unusual as you might think. It finds resonance in the well-publicized comments of Penn Jillete, the atheist, illusionist and comedian: 'I don't respect people who don't proselytize. I don't respect that at all. If you believe that there's heaven and hell and people could be going to hell and not getting eternal life or whether, and you think that it's not really worth telling them this because it would make it socially awkward... How much do you have to hate somebody to believe that everlasting life is possible and not tell them that?' Comments like these should cause every Christian to examine his conscience to see if he truly believes that Jesus is, as He said, 'the way, and the life....'"

The essence of looking into the results of the research work of Larry Alex Taunton so deeply lies in the fact that Satanism and cult religions can grow from and within the church in such a subtle way. Secondly it explained the fact that unbelief in Almighty God or any other gods is a religion on its own. What is also noteworthy in these findings are the attitudes of the young atheists, who unknown to them practice Satanism or cult religion in a subtle manners. The subtle manner often leads them into reading lots of satanic literatures that often take them from one level of Satanism or cult religion into another.

Also noteworthy in these findings are the arguments that are usually posed by atheists. They often make comments that provoke arguments. These arguments can sway a young Christian convert but matured Christians have what it takes to meet up to the challenge. Young converts, therefore, need to grow into spiritual maturity by personally studying the Bible, preferably New King James Version.

More often than not, Satanists especially those in the cloaks of Christians distort the central truth in the Bible by agreeing with some truths and placing some lies in between the truths. They are good at asking questions that can confuse and misdirect young Christian coverts who do not diligently study the Bible.

The other common characteristic of Satanism and cult

religions is manipulation. Satanists always seek and groom intelligent people who will be used to mislead others. With proper amount of brainwashing through philosophy, satanic literatures and other things, a cult leader is trained on how to manipulate others. The Bible confirms this in 2Timothy 3:13, which says, *"But evil men and seducers shall wax worse and worse, deceiving, and being deceived."*

Going by Henry Makow's interview with Svalis and results of other findings, Satanists train generational Satanists usually in military techniques and other professions. In other to manipulate the Christendom and manipulate public opinions about politics, religions, social and economic welfare, Satanists train and sponsor their members to become lawyers that will change the course of politics. Barack Obama did a lot of things in his support for abortion and gay bills that are against the teachings of the Bible during his tenure as the President of the United Sates.

Satanists also train journalists who will pervert the truth through the media and support anti-Christ policies, clergymen are also brought up to occupy sensitive positions in Churches, especially the ones with large congregation and big denominations like the Catholics, Anglicans, Methodists and a host of others. Of course, this does not mean that all the clergymen in these denominations or congregation are Satanists but the truth is most of them are planted there by Satanists. If a Catholic Pope like Joseph Ratzinger is proved to be a Satanist, there is no need to wonder at the number of Catholic priests that are proved to be paedophiles or Satanists as they are reported in the news.

Well trained Satanists are good at hiding their identities in order to manipulate and enlist others into cult religions. They and all the leaders of cult religions are usually intelligent and sufficiently brainwashed into believing that Satan is the godhead as in the story of Zeus and Kronos. This myth and other stories of the legends, gods and goddess had been made into movies and cartoons with sole objective of brainwashing.

The subliminal messages in movies, cartoons, music and every other means of entertainment, information and education are actually intended to wipe away the truth about God and the deity of Jesus in case anyone comes across it.

The question to address here is: how much truths do people know in the midst of web of lies, deceptions and manipulations?

Since at this stage, it is expected that readers understand the fact that the Bible is the only truth humanity has and the only tool they can use to sail through the ocean of insanity that is created by the devils. Even then, Satanists have attempted in several ways to change some truths in the Bible by manipulating some so called Christian denominations to have their own versions of the Bible. Such denominations like Jehovah Witness, Catholic, Mommons and so many others have their own Bibles which left out some central truths like the deity of Jesus Christ, hell or heaven. The truth in the original Christian Bible is perverted with additional materials like the apocryphal books in Catholic Bible. Such additional materials give room for the practice of Satanism like praying for the dead, which is contrary to the central truth in Hebrew 9:27. The passage says, *"And as it is appointed unto men once to die, but after this the judgment..."*

Some cult religions in disguise of Christianity also make use of scent to drive away unholy spirits and practice the Old Testament type sacrifices that had been abolished by the sacrifice of the Lamp of God called Jesus Christ. When a Christian denomination is involved in any of these types of things, it is proof that Satanism is practiced in subtle way though the people may not realize it.

While addressing the question of truth in the midst of webs of lies, Jesus said something crucial in Matthew 7:15-20, *"Beware of false prophets, which come to you in sheep's clothing, but inwardly they are ravening wolves. You shall know them by their fruits. Do men gather grapes of thorns, or figs of thistles? Even so every good tree brings forth good fruit; but a corrupt tree brings forth evil fruit. A good tree cannot bring forth evil fruit, neither can a corrupt tree bring forth good fruit. Every tree that brings not forth good fruit is hewn down, and cast into the fire. Wherefore by their fruits you shall know them."*

Going by the clue given by Jesus on how to distinguish Satanists (bad tree) from real Christians (good tree), the fruits each of them bears will differentiate them. When you weigh the followings in line with Bible: (i) the conduct or the ways of life (ii) the mood of worship (iii) the attitude (iv) the dressing (v) the language, you will get a clue if a person is a Satanist or Christian.

The good news is that it is easy to know who a typical Satanist is but the bad news is: it is hard if not impossible to detect a Satanist who uses Christianity a cover up unless you are filled with the Holy Spirit and the word of God.

A Christian does not need to be concerned about who or who is not a Satanist so as not to be judgmental or biased. All the Christian should be concerned about are found in Psalms Chapter One verses one to three, which says, *"Blessed is the man that walks not in the counsel of the ungodly, nor stands in the way of sinners, nor sits in the seat of the scornful. But his delight is in the law of the LORD; and in his law does he meditate day and night. And he shall be like a tree planted by the rivers of water, that brings forth his fruit in his season; his leaf also shall not wither; and whatsoever he does shall prosper."*

These are itemized as follow:

(i) Genuine Christians must not mix up with Satanists and must not mingle Satanism with Christianity. The Bible establishes one of the reasons for this in 1 Corinthians 15:33 which says, *"Be not deceived: evil company corrupt good manners."*

(ii) They must regularly study the Bible, obey and meditate on what they study. Through this they build and develop relationships with God, growing into maturity. The Bible says in 1 Peter 2:2. *"As newborn babes, desire the sincere milk of the word, that ye may grow thereby..."*

(iii) Genuine Christians bring forth good fruits which are fruits of the Spirit of God that are recorded in Galatians 5:22 and 23. The passage says, *"But the fruit of the Spirit is love, joy, peace, longsuffering, gentleness, goodness, faith, Meekness, temperance: against such there is no law."*

(iv) Christians must always not do good to others like preaching the Gospel and sharing their things with needy people commits sin, according to James 4:17. The passage says, *"Therefore to him that knows to do good, and does it not, to him it is sin."* All Christians must always seek for other people to be saved from Satan and devils who are determined to destroy mankind in hell.

A lot of things depend on studying and obeying the word of God, which include but not limited to the followings:

(i) It is through faith in the word of God can anyone get eternal life in heaven. In 1 Peter 1:23-25, the Bible says, *"Being born again, not of corruptible seed, but of incorruptible, by the word of God, which lives and abides forever. For all flesh is as grass, and all the glory of man as the flower of grass. The grass withers, and the flower thereof falls away: But the word of the Lord endures forever. And this is the word which by the gospel is preached unto you."*

(ii) It is through strict obedience and the use of the word of God can anyone overcome evil things, including battles of life like the one to be treated in the final chapter of this book. The word of God is the only weapon to fight evils, according to Ephesians 6:17. Verses 11 to 18 says, *"Put on the whole armour of God, that you may be able to stand against the wiles of the devil. For we wrestle not against flesh and blood, but against principalities, against powers, against the rulers of the darkness of this world, against spiritual wickedness in high places. Wherefore take unto you the whole armour of God, that ye may be able to withstand in the evil day, and having done all, to stand. Stand therefore, having your loins girt about with truth, and having on the breastplate of righteousness; And your feet shod with the preparation of the gospel of peace; Above all, taking the shield of faith, wherewith ye shall be able to quench all the fiery darts of the wicked. And take the helmet of salvation, and the sword of the Spirit, which is the word of God: Praying always with all prayer and supplication in the Spirit, and watching thereunto with all perseverance and supplication for all saints..."*

(iii) Through following the Bible, other people can easily read the word of God in the lives of Christians and be attracted to Christianity. The Bible says in 2 Corinthians 3:2 and 3, *"You are our epistle written in our hearts, known and read of all men: Forasmuch as you are manifestly declared to be the epistle of Christ ministered by us, written not with ink, but with the Spirit of the living God; not in tables of stone, but in fleshy tables of the heart."*

CHAPTER THIRTEEN

<u>THE BATTLE BETWEEN CHRISTIANS AND SATANISTS</u>

In the entire book of revelation, the battle and the struggle against Satan and his spirit warriors were revealed to John. In chapter 16 verses 13 to 16, *"And I saw three unclean spirits like frogs come out of the mouth of the dragon, and out of the mouth of the beast (anti-Christ), and out of the mouth of the false prophet. For they are the spirits of devils, working miracles, which go forth unto the kings of the earth and of the whole world, to gather them to the battle of that great day of God Almighty. Behold, I come as a thief. Blessed is he that watches, and keeps his garments, lest he walk naked, and they see his shame. And he gathered them together into a place called in the Hebrew tongue Armageddon."*

Here is the picture of how Satan organized himself, his warriors and the battle plan. Note his prototype of God's plans.

Satan, just as he planned in heaven before he was thrown out, assumes the position of God, The Father in this world. He introduces the beast who is the anti-Christ as his son just as Jesus Christ came into the world as The Son of God. This anti-Christ is to come as human being just as Jesus Christ came as man. The anti-Christ may be seen as human but it will actually be a demonic beast.

The spirits or devils operate in the lives of people just as Holy Spirit operates in Christians after they believe in Jesus Christ. When they are baptized and filled with the Holy Spirit, they begin to excise powers as children of God, according to John 1:12. As pointed earlier, Christians need to grow from babes into maturity so as to become soldiers of Christ who is equipped with the whole armour of God as in Ephesians 6:11-18. Anyone who is not a soldier of Christ can easily fall in the battlefield. For this reason the Bible says in 2Timothy 2:2-4, *"And the things that you have heard of me among many witnesses, the same commit them to faithful men, who shall be able to teach others also. You therefore must endure hardness, as a good soldier of Jesus Christ. No man that wars entangles himself with the affairs of this life; that he may please him who has chosen him to be a soldier."*

There is no in-between or neutral ground in this battle. Everyone (whether a child or adult) is either a soldier of Jesus Christ or working for Satan. In 1 John 2: 18-23, the Bible says, *"Little children, it is the last time: and as you have heard that anti-Christ shall come, even now are there many anti-Christs; whereby we know that it is the last time. They went out from us, but they were not of us; for if they had been of us, they would no doubt have continued with us: but they went out, that they might be made manifest that they were not all of us. But you have an unction from the Holy One, and you know all things. I have not written unto you because you know not the truth, but because you know it, and that no lie is of the truth. Who is a liar but he that denies that Jesus is the Christ? He is anti-Christ, that denies the Father and the Son. Whosoever denies the Son, the same has not the Father: (but) he that acknowledges the Son has the Father also."*

The above passage establishes the fact that anyone who denies the truth about Jesus Christ is an anti-Christ and an anti-Christ is a Satanist. The battle between Christians and Satanists or anti-Christ actually began in heaven, going by the book of Revelation chapter 12 verses 7 to 9. The Bible says in the passage, *"And there was war in heaven: Michael and his angels fought against the dragon; and the dragon fought and his angels, And prevailed not; neither was their place found any more in heaven. And the great dragon was cast out, that old serpent, called the Devil, and Satan, which deceives the whole world: he was cast out into the earth, and his angels were cast out with him."*

As at the time Satan and other angels fell from heaven up to the days of Noah, the Bible still addressed the fallen angels as spirits or sons of God, going by the history of creation and destruction of the world with water. In Genesis chapter 1 verses 1 and 2, the Bible says, *"in the beginning God created the heaven and the earth. And the earth was without form, and void; and darkness was upon the face of the deep. And the Spirit of God moved upon the face of the waters."*

Going by what happened in chapter 3 of the book of Genesis, it is certain that the devil had been thrown away from heaven before the earth was recreated. Also from the passage about the history of creation, the earth had been in existence when the devils and the angels were thrown out of heaven. They hovered above the earth, probably looking for where to dwell. When God recreated the earth and handed it over to man in Genesis chapter 2, the devil took it from him in chapter 3.

With the devil ruling the world, it is a lot easy for him and other fallen angels to mingle with the affairs of mankind. In Genesis chapter 6 verses 1 to 8, the devils went to the extreme by raising children with the daughters of men. In verses 1 and 2, the Bible says, *"And it came to pass, when men began to multiply on the face of the earth, and daughters were born unto them, That the sons of God saw the daughters of men that they were fair; and they took them wives of all which they chose."*

After these fallen angels had gone that far, they began to raise giants on the earth whose deeds and thoughts were wicked continuously, according to verse 5. It is likely that it is about this time that the legends stories about gods or goddesses or demigods began. These children of the fallen angels are apparently no ordinary human beings. Hence they oppressed and did whatever wickedness they can conceive. At the end of it all, God decided to wipe out the entire perverted creation, preserving Noah and his family with pairs of each other creatures in an ark.

In 1993, CBS aired a television special entitled "The Incredible Discovery of Noah's Ark", which according to some analysis is the final installment of the mysteries of the ancient world. The documentary about the Biblical Noah's Ark takes an in-depth look at the history and ambiguity of this Biblical symbol that is said to have rescued two of every animal during a great worldwide food.

In May 1, 2010, Benjamin Radford in News Discovery wrote a short history of Noah's Ark discoveries as follows:

"Last week an organization called Noah's Ark Ministries called a press conference in Hong Kong to announce that they had made one of the most significant archaeological discoveries in history. Yeung Wing-Cheung claims he and his research team located the remains of Noah's Ark on Turkey's Mount Ararat.

"Yeung says that wood samples taken from the site were carbon-dated to about 5,000 years ago, and that he is 99

percent certain that it is Noah's Ark based on historical accounts, including the Bible and local beliefs of the people in the area, as well as dating...

"The great explorer Marco Polo wrote around 1300 in his book The Travels Of Marco Polo that 'in the heart of great Armenia is a very high mountain shaped like a cube (or cup), on which Noah's ark is said to have rested, whence it is called 'The Mountain Of Noah's Ark.'

"Yeung is not the first person to claim to have found the ark; in fact Noah's Ark has been discovered at least a half-dozen times in the past 50 years. While many believe the story of Noah's Ark is merely a fable, some are convinced that the Bible is literally true, and finding the Ark is merely a matter of time. Interests in the ark spiked in the 1970s after a man named Georgie Hagopian said he located and climbed on the remains of the ark at least twice... Of course while extracting facts about this discovery, it is realized that a good number of people scoff at it just as many have scoffed at the Bible mockingly calling it 'arkeology'."

This is to be expected because one of the most effective weapons of Satan against mankind is unbelief. Because of this and so many other weapons that had earlier been discussed, relating the truth in the midst of web of lies becomes a great task. Despite all the proofs of the reality of life, death, hell and heaven, including outstanding testimonies of some people who had gone through Near-Death Experiences, so many still do not belief the gospel truth of the Bible. A lot of people erroneously think that they would be pardoned for their ignorance but the Bible makes us to understand in Hosea 4: 6 that people can perish out of ignorance. The case is like a man who drives his sports car on a one way at top speed out of ignorance that the road is one way. Another man drives from the opposite direction without the knowledge of the speeding sports car. Just because both of them are ignorance of the danger ahead of them does not prevent the accident. It is also not enough for them to know about the danger, each of them must do something to avoid getting involved in the accident. In the same way, just because a man is ignorance of the of the lake fire of fire which the Bible talks about in Revelation 21:8 cannot stop him from ending up there. Similarly, the knowledge of hell is not enough to stop a man from going there. He must do something about it if he really does not want to end up there.

Jesus makes the people to understand how easy it is to get to hell in Matthew 7:13-14. He says, *"Enter by the narrow gate: for the wide is the gate and broad is the way that leads to destruction, and there are many who go in by it. Because narrow is the gate and difficult is the way which leads to life, and there are few who finds it."*

The question to address now is: what makes it difficult for people to find the way to eternal life in heaven? The answer is not farfetched. Humanity has an arch enemy called Satan who makes it difficult if not impossible for people to find their way to heaven through Jesus Christ. He is still furious that he lost out the battle in heaven. He and the rest of the fallen angels who are now called the devils or demons have no other place to live for all eternity but hell. So he and the rest of the devils are working round the clock to ensure that only few people make it to heaven, if at all anyone would get there. This is the basis of what Jesus said in Matthew 11:12 *"And from the days of John the Baptist until now the kingdom of heaven suffers violence, and the violent take it by force."*

Satan designs so many ways as decoys and so many things as weapons and tools to lure people to hell. Such ways of decoys are religions of all kinds, including the ones that pose as Christianity. Some of the weapons and tools of mass eternal destructions are fornication in subtle or extreme method, materialism, violence and every other thing that are directly or indirectly opposed to the word of God.

Mankind cannot resist these decoys, weapons and tools; especially when most people are ignorant of the real way, the truth and the life which are in Jesus, according to what He said in John 14:6. Satan and the devils make the kingdom of God (heaven) a place to be possessed only through struggles and battles. First, man has to struggle and subdue his flesh through prayers and sometimes fasting, walking in the spirit as Galatians 5:16 instructed. By walking in the flesh, according to Galatians 5:19-21, man walks away from the kingdom of God right from this world, courting with eternal death in hell. In Romans 8:6, the Bible says, *"For to be carnally minded is (second) death (in hell according to*

Revelation 21:8), but to be spiritually minded is (eternal) life and peace in heaven (Revelation 21:4)."

The weapons and tools the devils use against humanity make life on earth a battle against the kingdom of darkness. The author attempts to explain this battle in two of his novels titled: "The Redeemer And The Dragon" and "The Battle Of The Conquerors". In these battles of life, Satan and his warriors who are, according to Ephesians 6:12, in the class of principalities; powers, rulers of darkness and host of wickedness fight everybody on earth. The battles never end until the person departs from the world to either in hell or heaven. The warriors of Satan or the fallen angels are mostly invisible, which makes the battle not visible to mankind and non-scientific but spiritual.

These warriors fight all humans according to their weakness and spiritual levels. The more matured the Christian, the more thorough the opposition. More often than not, many people made themselves available to be used as vessels by Satan to fight against or even kill fellow humans. Thus those who are not spiritually inclined would readily consider these vessels as enemies but the author's above novels prove that *"no mortal is an enemy of mortal"*. It is the immortal and invisible enemies of mortals that use mortals against other mortals.

There is a case study of a Christian woman who was involved in a motor accident in Nigeria that can be used to give a picture of the danger humanity faces every second of every day of human life.

She was among the fourteen passengers in the bus that tumbled on the expressway between the two cities of Lagos and Ibadan in Nigeria. About eight people died on the spot with blood gushing out of the bodies of both the dead people and those who are alive. Only this Christian woman seemed to sustain minor injury. The rest were either dead or in bad shape or in need of medical attention. She sat down beside the road as the members of road safety corps cleared the dead, taking the wounded to the nearest state hospital. There was substantial amount of blood on the road as the woman watched with awe, wondering how easy it was to lose one's life.

According to her testimony, as she was in deep thoughts

about the way the accident occurred, she noticed a snail crawling to the part of the road that was filled with human blood. It appeared to be licking the blood, making the woman to suspect that the snail was not ordinary type. She went to grab the snail and put it in her bag and later in a small container. A moment later, one satanic looking man came out from the bush, glaring at the woman with frustration. That instant moment, the woman suspected that the man must have caused the accident so that he could have the snail to leak blood of the victims.

With courage and curiosity, the woman got another vehicle that would take her home without handling over the snail. She wanted to frustrate the plan of the man and know what would become of the snail that licked the blood of human beings. She kept the container in the kitchen when she got home. She had almost completely forgotten about it until the following day. When she got to the kitchen to prepare meal in the morning, the snail has turned into lots of money. She frantically ran out of the house, calling the people's attention to what happened.

The following things need to be considered about this case:

Firstly, most people including some Christians are very ignorant of the battles around them despite proofs of demonic operations and the spiritual battles. When some people become conscious of these battles through what happened to them or others, they run to wrong places or people like false prophets or Satanists for protection instead of going to the Lord Jesus in prayers and hold Him by His words in the Bible.

Secondly, unknown to most people, there are only two opposing human soldiers which are Christian soldiers and the Satan's human soldiers. Since the Bible has established the fact that all Christians are soldiers of Christ in 2 Timothy 2:3-4, they need to wear the whole armour of war as in Ephesians 6: 10-20 before they can tackle various levels of warriors of Satan. While Satan and his warriors mostly use humans (Satanists) to engage other people, especially Christians in physical battles (as it can be noted in the case of the woman and the snail), the spirit warriors actually operate in the realm of the spirit to bring about supernatural manifestations. For instance Satanists can conjure a demon that appears like the spirit of the dead. The powers of Christians who are well grounded in the word of God are far superior to the powers of Satanists, devils and Satan himself. In 2 Corinthians 10: 4-5, the Bible says of the Christian soldiers, *"For the weapons of our warfare are not carnal, but mighty through God to the pulling down of strong holds; Casting down imaginations, and every high thing that exalts itself against the knowledge of God, and bringing into captivity every thought to the obedience of Christ..."*

Top Satanists know that Christians are the real threats to their religions and their plans to rule the world. As long as there are Christians in this world, Satan knows he and those who follow him cannot succeed in the plan to bring about one world, one identity, one religion and one ordinance to him. Satanists like the freemasons and illuminati had been planning to take over the world from one generation right into another without success. The reason they fail is because Christian soldiers never stop resisting them with the power of God, which is not carnal but mighty to the pulling down of stronghold. Without knowing it, Satanists accept the Lordship of Jesus Christ by bowing and postponing their endless plan to take over the world. In Philippians 2: 9-11, the Bible says, *"Therefore God also has highly exalted him, and given him a name which is above every name: That at the name of Jesus every knee should bow, of things in heaven, and things in earth, and things under the earth; And that every tongue should confess that Jesus Christ is Lord, to the glory of God the Father."*

Every spirit acknowledges the Lordship of Jesus Christ whenever His name is mentioned. There are so many Satanists who confirm this fact after getting converted. Everybody that accepts the dating period in the world acknowledges the fact that Jesus is the Christ was born at BC (Before Christ) and died at AD (After Death). Humanity consciously or unconsciously recognizes the fact that Jesus Christ is the Messiah, according to Isaiah 9:6-7, which says, *"For unto us a child is born, unto us a son is given: and the government shall be upon his shoulder: and his name shall be called Wonderful, Counsellor, The mighty God, The everlasting Father, The Prince of Peace. Of the increase of his government and peace there shall be no end, upon the throne of David, and upon his kingdom, to order it, and to establish it with judgment and with justice from henceforth even forever. The zeal of the LORD of hosts will perform this."*

If at all most people think they do not accept the Lordship of Jesus Christ now, when He comes the second time to take His people home as indicated in 1 Thessalonians 4:16-18, everybody will accept that Jesus is the Lord over all. By then, of course, it would be too late. The Bible says in that passage, *"For the Lord himself shall descend from heaven with a shout, with the voice of the archangel, and with the trump of God: and the dead in Christ shall rise first: Then we which are alive and remain shall be caught up together with them in the clouds, to meet the Lord in the air: and so shall we ever be with the Lord. Therefore comfort one another with these words."*

It is after the real Christians had been taken away from this world that the reign of anti-Christ will begin. If it is taking violence to get to the kingdom of God at this period, it is certain that it will take much more spiritually violent people to survive the reign of anti-Christ. So it is wise to go to Jesus Christ now and accept him as Lord and Saviour of your soul. When you do that, you actually declare yourself as a child of God who will be given the power of a child of God, according to John 1: 12. When you become a child of God, you begin to grow into a Christian soldier that is sure to become a conqueror in the battle. The Bible says in Romans 8:35-39, *"Who shall separate us from the love of Christ? shall tribulation, or distress, or persecution, or famine, or nakedness, or peril, or sword? As it is written, For thy sake we are killed all the day long; we are accounted as sheep for the slaughter. No, in all these things we are more than conquerors through him that loved us. For I am persuaded, that neither death, nor life, nor angels, nor principalities, nor powers, nor things present, nor things to come, Nor height, nor depth, nor any other creature, shall be able to separate us from the love of God, which is in Christ Jesus our Lord."*

BOOKS BY THE SAME AUTHOR: DIPO TOBY ALAKIJA, Published By Calvary Rock Publishing and Resources, Available At www.amazon.com

The Weight Of Death

Dipo Toby Alakija's story Of The Spirit Eyes

PLAY ONE: HORROR IN THE FAMILY: Talimi probably did not envisage his death when he was trying to compel his son, Damola to succeed him in the occult Brotherhood. Other members of the secret cult were aware of the battle between them. So when Talimi died; his family, especially Damola who was a diehard Christian began to fall prey to the cult. Using all their powers and the spirit that posed as Talimi's ghost, the cult waged war against the family, tormenting and making them to be at loggerheads.

PLAY TWO: RITUAL KIDS' KIDNAPPERS: Victor and the rest of the members of the School Bible Club were taught that there are lots of evil people in this world but he did not understand why God allowed him to be among the children that were taken away from their parents. He soon understood that he was to be used by God to rescue other children who did not know that everyone that truly believes in Jesus has the power to overcome evil.

PLAY THREE: THE WEIGHT OF DEATH: Awoseun would not have known the real source of problems of mankind if his father had not given him the power to see demons tormenting the people in different ways. What he was yet to know, however, was the power of light over darkness. When he was caught in crossfire between these powers, he desperately sought for deliverance.

The Redeemer And The Dragon

The Epic Of Three Kingdoms

Dragon, the king of Doom kingdom gets the legal right to rule over the kingdom of man when First Couple breaks the Law Of Dominion and turns all the mortals into his slaves. When The Father who creates all the kingdoms sends The Redeemer to deliver them, Brethren is selected as one of the few giant warriors that will terrorize Dragon and the rulers of darkness in the decisive battle between Eternity kingdom and Doom kingdom over eternal destinations of the people. Because The Redeemer counts on the mortal warriors called Believers to deliver the rest of the slaves, he equips them with The Word and Comforter who teaches them all things. However, a warrior of Dragon called Ignorance blindfolds vast majority of the people and makes them oblivious of the battlefields in The Flesh, The Mind and The Spirit. Since most of these mortals cannot see beyond their immediate environments, the enemies get the chance to lead them on the path of Doom kingdom which is a place of eternal agony, making the battle on the way to Eternity kingdom of The Father so fierce that only the violent Believers can get to the place.

Footsteps In The Mud
A 13-Episode Drama Package

The 13-Episode drama book involves Bosede who learnt many wrong things from her parents' conduct and foul language. She was forced to marry Kola when she became pregnant. Using her mother's method to handle her father, she tried to subject Kola to her control. In the course of that, she made life terrible for him. Although her mother tried to warn her of the implications of maltreating her husband but Bosede has grown out of control. Consequently, while looking for peace, Kola was pushed out of the house. He made friends with some guys who taught him the unholy ways of life and influenced him to become a menace in the house.

Junior who was born at time the couple never proved to be responsible parents also learnt wrong things from them. He decided to follow his father's footsteps by taking alcohol when he was in primary school. As if that was not bad enough, he tried to teach other children in the school the madness in his home. A school teacher, however, was able to influence him and his mother by teaching them Christian morals. Even then, Junior was soon caught in the crossfire at home as his father tried to enlist him as a future member of a secret cult that posed as a social club.

No More Tears To Shed

Kidnappers took Tokunbo away from his grandparents in a city in Nigeria when he was a little boy. A nice woman found him in another town and gave him a false identity. She spoilt him with love, making him to grow into a rebellious teenager that was not appreciated anywhere.

When Janet made him a Christian, however, life began to make sense to him until the day he was beaten to the point of death for the offence he knew nothing about. He left the town for the city which, unknown to him, held his true identity and the link to his parents in the United States. To find them was only a question of time.

The Unromantic Love Birds

They were very much in love right from their school days but when they got married and had children, romance became the game Charles' wife refused to play. No matter how much he tried to make her understand the unbearable condition her unromantic attitude has subjected him into, she would not change. Consequently, after enduring for so long, he was forced to look for the women that would make up for her weakness. He unofficially married a beautiful lady of insane jealousy. Though she was ready to give him what was missing in his marriage, it soon dawn on him that he has solved one big problem only to create a bigger one.

Bloodshed In Campus

A poor widow tearfully warned her son, Richard, against joining the bad wagon when he got an admission into one of the Nigerian Universities. He resisted the membership of groups of students, including the Christian Fellowship until he had an encounter with a member of The Black Skulls - a deadly and ruthless secret cult on campus. Before Richard knew what he was up against, the head of The Black Skulls had arranged items for his initiation into the cult. While resisting being initiated, he ran to the Christian Fellowship for help. The leader of the Christian Fellowship dragged The President of Students' Union Government (S.U.G) into the conflict. With the involvement of the S.U.G President, another formidable cult called The Red Eyes felt obliged to team up against The Black Skulls. Then the campus turned into a battlefield and BLOODSHED became the order of the black day.

Ransom For Love
A Collection Of Three Plays

She accepted his marriage proposal without knowing the kind of person he was. She soon discovered that he was a mean and ruthless guy who was always ready to get whatever he wanted by all means even if he has to pay for it with the lives of others. She was in his bondage, especially when her parents who believed he was a generous and gentleman were on his side. Because she considered the proposal to marry him as a marriage engagement with the devil incarnate, she decided that she would rather die than to share her life with him. Then out of the blues, this passionate gentleman sneaked into her life despite all she did to discourage him. She could not resist his love for her when he offered to set her free from the devil incarnate. Then the battle began - sooner than they anticipated.

<u>The Battle Of The Conquerors</u>

Wickedness takes over the land of Bondage from First Couple and subjects everybody into slavery without giving anybody the chance to be free. Love brings The Redeemer from Eternity and offers the slaves the chance to escape. Wickedness soon declares war and engages everyone in the battle. The Redeemer makes the redeemed people Conquerors by giving them the armour of war and Comforter but Wickedness cannot be undone. He has several thousands of years of experience in the war. So he is quick to recognize the weakness

of the redeemed people who are ignorant of their strengths and advantages. Although the Conquerors fight like immutable giants, rescuing victims of war, many people suffer heavy casualties. Since King Wickedness knows that a redeemed person is strong enough to chase one thousand of his warriors at a time, and two would put ten thousand into flight, he enlists as one of his warriors the people's deadliest enemy called Disunity. Wickedness is able to strike the people by making them to fight with one another, turning what is supposed to be their best moments in the battle into tales of woes.

<u>The Insanity Of Humanity</u>

The Dumbing Down Of Humanity

Man is made to exercise his freewill. The mind of his own and the power to choose between right and wrong, good and evil, light and darkness is about to be washed away through brainwashing. The agents of control dubbed as Secret Government by John Todd (the top Illuninati defector) have put necessary machinery in place to ensure that all human beings are in conformity

in their thinking and ways of life, trying to wipe away diversity, which makes each person unique. This book attempts to shed light on how the techniques of mind control are applied through the use of propaganda, education, entertainments, drugs, religions, media and other means of communications. It is the result of research works, some of which are based on findings of various researchers and writers like Wes Penre, Bugger Lugz, Edward Hunter, Hadley Cantril, Herbert Krugman, David L. Robb, Vaughan Bell, Juliana Gomez, Ryan Duffy Vice, Henry Makow, David Nicholls, Fritz Springmeire, Steven Hassan, Renate Thienel, Debra Pursell, Mary Pride and a host of others whose works are acknowledged in this book

Network Bible Club Youth And Adult Story Book

A Collection Of 26 Stories, 26 Poems 26 Hymn tuned Songs And Bible Lessons

The issue of moral instructions in schools and at homes is threatened with extinction. Consequently, so many youths are involved in prostitution, drug addictions, cultism, fraudulent practices, armed robberies and other crimes. Those who are supposed to be trained as leaders in various walks of life are the ones posing serious threats to many lives. Many parents who fail to add moral values to the upbringing of their children often times breed potential criminals under their roofs without knowing it. Apart from these, many other people negatively influence young ones through the media, music, publications, films, conduct and foul language; making them to lose their moral and family values. This book one just like the rest of other volumes is an attempt to bring back moral instructions into schools and campuses through the use of stories, hymn tuned songs, poems, Bible lessons and class activities. It is designed to assist teachers and ministers in Secondary Schools, Bible Clubs, Churches and Campus Fellowships to teach people, especially youths the Word of God and serves as a school text book in subjects relating to literature, music and other creative works.

Foundation Bible Club A-Z Story Book

A Collection Of Stories, Bible Lessons, Nursery Rhymes And Songs

An adage says, "a man who builds a house without building his child builds what the child will later sell." Proverbs 22:6 says, "train up a child in the way he should go: and when he is old, he will not depart from it." This book is an attempt to assist parents and teachers to meet up to the challenges that befall them in carrying out this important function in the light of the moral decadence that is prevailing all over the world. The first edition of the book was used by several thousands of teachers, ministers and parents in schools, Churches and homes to build the moral values of young ones. Apart from the stories, songs and Bible passages for the young ones to study, there is a seminar material that is based on the lecture which the author delivered to school proprietors, children ministers and Christian professionals in this volume.

The Young Generation Bible Club Story Book

A Collection Of Stories, Poems And Bible Lessons

Although this book serves as a follow-up to the stories and lessons in Foundation Bible Club A-Z Story Book, it is a separate academic; evangelical and Ministration tool to reach out and teach young ones in primary and junior high schools. Just like other volumes, it contains stories, songs, poems, Bible lessons and class activities that can be used by parents and ministers at homes, Churches, Schools, Bible Clubs and other Fellowships. It is a manual that assists them in boosting the moral values of children of all age groups in the modern days that are characterized with brainwashing information, ungodly teaching materials and entertainments. Apart from the contents for the young ones, there are also lectures and tips on how to effectively use the book to raise God-fearing children. All the published volumes of the book are used by hundreds of thousands of parents, teachers, ministers and other Christian professionals.

Successful Christianity And Basic Ministries

A Collection Of Christian Resource Materials

The first question is how Christianity is practiced even in a hostile environment. Next to that is the question about the potentials of Christians in spite of their apparent limitations. The other issues are connected to the successes, deliverance, callings, basic ministries of all Christians and evangelism. Various schools of thoughts have attempted these questions but many answers only portray Christianity as a form of religion instead of a way of life as specified by God. Some answers give room for compromise, hypocrisies, dogmas and denominational doctrines. The misconceptions about these areas of Christianity have brought about worldliness instead of righteousness and false achievements instead of fulfillment. This book which contains six different subjects had been used to hold seminars at various levels, train ministers and Christian workers in Bible Schools and to equip the Church. It explains in simple terms the seemingly complex issues on practice of Christianity, Potentials, Deliverance, God's Kind Of Success, Evangelism and Basic Ministries of a Christian with Biblical principles, life transforming stories and illustrations.

Christian Ministries And Basic Leadership

A Collection Of Christian Resource Materials

As it is common to say that the hood does not make a monk, the dignified positions and bogus titles of many Christian leaders in modern days do not really make them Gospel Ministers. This course book - a compilation of five resource materials on Missions And Outreach Ministries, Christian Communication Arts, Christian Leadership, Christian Education Methodology and Ministries Of Improvisations - aims at making every matured Christian an effective minister and leader at their respective homes, in communities and nations. It teaches various ways Christians can meet up to their responsibilities and commitments as ministers and leaders that reconcile people to God and edify the Body Of Christ, reaching out to souls at the same time. All of the resource materials are in use in Bible Schools like College Of Christian Education And Missions, Churches and other ministries to raise Christian workers, Evangelists, Missionaries and other Ministers that serve at various levels and leadership capacities.

Christian Communications And Human Resources

A Collection Of Christian Resource Materials

The world is not in need of those who will fix errors of humanity but in dire need of matured Christians that would use their gifts to communicate the word of God and lead their families, the Church, communities and their countries in the way of righteousness. Very few of them, however, seem to have what it takes to take their positions as leaders and ministers in their spheres despite their God-given potentials. Thus this Course Book - a compilation of five resource materials on Christian Oral Communications, Christian Drama Communications, Christian Musical Communications, Christian Human Resources and Children Evangelism - makes serious attempts to introduce everybody into various creative ministries that are required in the Body of Christ and in the world. It teaches in a simple manner the management of human resources and the ways Christians can use their gifts to reach out to souls through speaking, writing, drama, media, musical and children ministries. The resource materials equip and help individuals to identify their callings, providing Biblical principles and guidelines on how to be effective and productive in the service of the Lord in spite of the hostile environments.

Calvary Rock Resource Booklet One
The Children Of God And The Slaves

This edition begins with children world where stories like "Ben, The Child Atheist", "Lola And The Bible" and "The Three Brave children" are used to teach children of all age groups about the existence of God and the need to study and obey the Bible. The article: "A critical Debate Between An Atheist Professor And His Christian Student" makes the youths and adults appreciate the passage in Psalm 14:1, which says, "a fool says in his heart, 'there is no God...'
" There are study articles like "The supreme God," "The Belief in reincarnation" with the major one: "The children of God And The slaves" which treat the issues of man existing in three parts: The Body, The Spirit and The soul. They expose the readers so the realm of the Spirits. Apart from the drama episode titled: "Going Haywire," there are evangelical materials like "Cheap And Expensive lies", "The woman with four Lovers," "Encounter with Demon from The Grave," "The Life That saves All" and other teaching stories and articles.

The Days Of Gross Darkness
Calvary Rock Resources Booklet Volume 2

The Children World exposes young minds to things of the spirit through creative use of poems, songs, illustrated stories and Bible lessons. The Youth World is also rich with edifying articles, poems and stories like: "Who Would Share My Burden?" and "Do You Take

This Woman As Your Beloved Wife?" The World Of Adults And Christian Professionals begins with the final message of Keith Green who died of plane crash, titled: "Why You Should Go To The Mission Field." The Christian Education Section treats the issue of Christians and Christianity. Next to that is adult story titled: "Lust Affairs" which is the second episode in the drama book titled: "Footsteps In The Mud." Another story titled: The Land That Has Lost Its Peace" follows the drama. Articles and tracts materials proceed

the main subject of "The Days Of Gross Darkness", which extensively teaches and illustrates the spiritually blindness of the modern world in spite of the increase of knowledge. Christian Education And Ministration Services Seminars titled: "Christian Leadership, "Christian Leadership Character", "Patterns; Principles And Power Of Delegation" and "Social Vices Destroy Lives" provide more teaching materials. Other articles and tract materials complement this edi*tion*.

<u>Spoil The Child, Destroy The Nation</u>

This collection of sixteen short educational dramas exemplifies the decadent lifestyles, especially among Nigerian youths as opposed to the family and national values that are portrayed in the pledge to the nation.

All the stories are based on some of the most intriguing cases that are studied at different times and locations in Nigeria.

While some dramas hold westernization through means of information and entertainments accountable for the near extinction of the major part of Nigerian values, others establish the fact that parents who spare their children from rigours of normal life often create out of them menaces that would pose serious threats to lives and properties in future. This parental factor also exposes young minds to life of luxuries instead of preparing them to face the huddles ahead of them.

The various issues that boil on the sources of social vices and crimes in Nigeria are so vividly presented in all the dramas that they can be imagined like motion pictures.

<u>AFRICANS IN BONDAGE</u>
<u>Book One: Africans Still In Fetters</u>

Patrice Emery Lumumba, Congo's First Prime Minister and President said at All-African Conference in 1960, "The Colonialists

138

care for nothing for Africa for her own sake. They are attracted by African riches and their actions are guided by the desire to preserve their interests in Africa against the wishes of the African people. For colonialists all means are good if they help them to possess these riches."

An African adage says; "if you close your eyes to facts, you will learn through accidents."

The above and so many other quotes which are used as emphases on the results of research works into the claims of some notable African leaders indicate that Western Nations are not as friendly as they seem right from the time of slave trade.

The playwright attempts to present the results of his research works on why African nations are never free from conflicts, economic, social and political servitude through the use of different academic papers that are treated in educational dramas with the titles "Grand Conspiracies Against Africa", "The Speeches Of Discord", "The Conspiracy Theory Of History", "The Brain Development Of A Child", "The Problem With Technology", "The Handover Of Legacy", "The Warmongering Nations", "The Slave Masters In Africa" and "Mothers: The Determinants Of Destinies" in book one.

Book Two: Spiritual Bondage

With studied cases that are peculiar to Africa, the author attempts to explain some mysteries relating to cultism; witchcraft; black magic and others. These dramas titled: "The Threats Of Cult Members On Campus", The Choice Of Death", "Lagidi: The Spirit Husband", "The Mirage Of A Marriage", "Truth Is The Weapon Of Freedom", "The Enemies Of Marriage", "The Wrath Of An Accuser" and "House Of God In A Mess" are mostly based on real life experiences. They paint vivid pictures of how the spirit realm can influence the physical world.

In God American Founding Fathers Trusted

Through absolute trust in God that characterized the early American leadership as virtuous and courageous, the founding fathers were able to secure independence from the British and build the United States into a vibrant nation. The teachings of the Bible so much influenced the leadership that John Adams, the 2nd President said, "we recognize no sovereign but God, and no King as Jesus!" Barely a century later, however, civil war broke out after an attempt

139

was made to assassinate Andrew Jackson, the 7th President during the Bank War. Other US Presidents like Abraham Lincoln (the 16th President) and John F. Kennedy (35th President) were not lucky enough to escape assassinations.

Thomas Jefferson, the 3rd President said, "Educate and inform the whole mass of people. Enable them to see that it is in their best interest to preserve peace and order, and they will preserve them". This book is an attempt of the author to help American citizens create peaceful instead of hostile environments through the studies and analyses of the quotes of the founding fathers, which are related to issues of Politics, Religions, Economies, Educations, American Values and Social Welfare.

The African Values And Legacies

Results of research works reveal that any nation that fails to orientate all categories of its citizens on what the country stands for and against gives rooms for other countries to devalue the national value, violate the law and order; deforming the prevailing norms and cultures in all the communities.

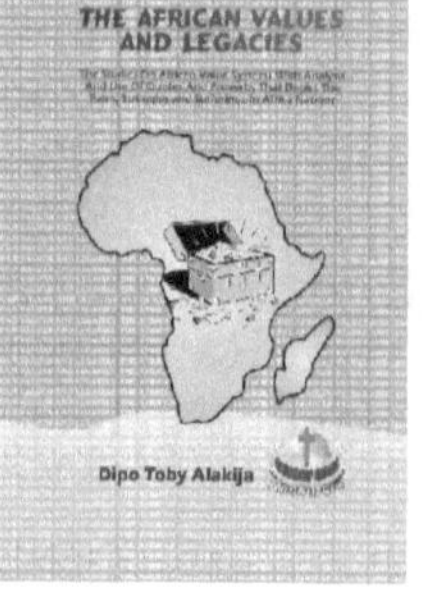

Most of African values, enriched with proverbs like "a goat is never pronounced innocent if the judge is a leopard" and "when brothers fight to death; a stranger inherits their father's estate", are getting eroded with westernization. The African heritages through the transfer of cultures, norms and order from one generation to another are threatened with extinctions since the time of colonization, particularly in oil-rich African nations.

The shutting down of value systems which are usually designed to boost moral values of citizens and enhance the functions of political, social and economic machineries are responsible for civil wars, terrorism, genocides and other atrocities in most African nations.

This book which is designed to be studied in African Tertiary Institutions shares the results of research works into the causes of conflicts, political and economic servitude in Africa; using the analyses of quotes of some of the notable leaders and African proverbs to reinforce the value systems on the continent.

The Stories And Studies Of African Values

Most African and other nations often build and develop economic, political and other structures at the expense of the Value Systems which are sometimes constructed by their National Anthems and The Pledge To The Nations. The neglect or shutting down of National Value Systems in these nations which arguably are the live wires that power other sectors within the societies give room for vices and crimes to be on the increase.

This book is designed to be studied by parents, teachers and students in primary or junior and high schools in Africa with the objectives of imbibing African traditional and moral values into them. With particular focus on children and youths, through the use of stories; poems; proverbs; quotes and class activities, the author attempts to give vivid pictures of African Values as opposed to westernization which is clearly wiping out what the founding fathers of the nations on the continent stand for.

Building Your Future As Young Africans

Going by world history, mankind is always faced with all kinds of challenges that are peculiar to each nation but the patriotic or unpatriotic attitudes of the citizens always determine if the country would overcome the problems or not.

Many African youths who see and feel the problems in their countries sometimes blame the Governments. Consequently, a lot of them are enlisted as rebels who often times fight against their Governments. They are also involved in crimes, terrorism and other atrocities without realizing their deadly implications in future.

Youths are often ignorant of the fact that what they do today will determine what their tomorrow and the future of their countries would be.

This book makes serious attempts to help both youths and adults in Africa to understand the normal process of real success through the resource materials inside.

The author explains how problems can be seen as opportunities to excel in life, using real life stories as cases for studies, quoting relevant authorities to buttress his points.

The book is also designed to teach African youths of the need to build their nations by encouraging them to enhance their values through skill acquisitions, setting goals and making best use of their potentials and the available resources.

www.ingramcontent.com/pod-product-compliance
Lightning Source LLC
Chambersburg PA
CBHW051451130726
47987CB00005B/2269